The Co-opera

GUIDE TO RUNNING YOUR SMALL BUSINESS

The Co-operative Bank
GUIDE TO RUNNING YOUR SMALL BUSINESS

DAVID S. PORTER

Holyoake Books

THE AUTHOR

David S. Porter LLB was born in 1942 and has lived in Bolton, Lancashire, all his life. Educated at Bolton Grammar School and Sedbergh, he studied law at Manchester University, obtaining a 2(i) Honours Degree. He was articled to a Manchester firm of solicitors and subsequently joined his father's practice, now Porter Hope & Knipe. His book *Financial Management for Solicitors* is in its third edition. He has lectured widely to the legal profession and to businessmen, and advised many small businesses in setting up and running their own concerns. He is married with three children and has done all his writing at home with the assistance of his wife. He is fully alive to the pressures of "after hours working", and to the everyday problems of running your own business.

CONTENTS

FOREWORD		vii
AUTHOR'S PREFACE		viii
CHAPTERS		
1	YOUR OWN BOSS?	1
2	STRUCTURE OF THE BUSINESS	9
3	HOW TO MAKE A PROFIT	15
4	FORECASTS AND BUDGETS	32
5	ANALYSIS	46
6	CASH FLOW	59
7	SOURCES OF FINANCE	73
8	TAXATION	77
9	MARKETING AND SELLING	81
Appendix A	Service Industry Model	100
Appendix B	Manufacturing Industry Model	115
Index		130

Holyoake Books is the imprint
of the Co-operative Union Limited,
Holyoake House, Hanover Street,
Manchester M60 0AS

First published May 1988

Copyright © David S. Porter 1988

British Library Cataloguing in Publication Data

Porter, David S.
    The Co-operative Bank guide to running
    your small business.
    1. Great Britain. Small firms. Financial
    management - Manuals
    I. Title II. Co-operative Bank
    658.1'592'0941

ISBN 0-85195-155-4

Printed and bound in Great Britain
by the Manchester Free Press
59 Whitworth Street, Manchester M1 3WT

FOREWORD

Setting up a new business or developing an existing one can be fraught with problems. However, under a new scheme, 'Lawyers for Enterprise', help is at hand in the form of your local solicitor. The scheme allows you to make an initial visit to your solicitor completely free of charge, so you've nothing to lose.

David Porter, a practising solicitor with 25 years' experience, has found that the initial problems facing new and small businesses relate more to the risk that the owner is being asked to take and underwrite than to purely financial problems. For example, a ten-year lease, even at a modest rent, is a substantial liability.

It is for this reason that he wrote this guide for The Co-operative Bank. He feels that anyone analysing their business problems by using this book will then have a much better chance of obtaining the right advice at the right price. I endorse that view.

Having read the book, what should you do next? Quite simply you should arrange to visit your solicitor in order to get more information about the areas with which you are having difficulties. The advice you receive will be neutral and, of course, your first visit won't cost you a penny.

I thoroughly recommend this book to all those people who already run a small business - and all those many other people who might be considering setting up a business.

Good reading and every success.

PETER WALKER

Head of Development,
Co-operative Bank plc.

AUTHOR'S PREFACE

It is some ten years since I wrote my first business book, *Financial Management for Solicitors* (now in its third edition), and it has become very clear that, apart from the product or services, there are basic rules common to all types of business large or small. Those rules can be easily assimilated and make the difference between coping and being dynamic. Business is not just about making money, but unfortunately you need enough to be able to succeed and to develop your particular skills.

All businesses are about risk and if it was easy everybody would be a millionaire. There is no point in making life difficult for yourself, however, and this book shows how you can develop your business ideas with the minimum amount of risk. Two sets of figures appear in the Appendices and in part throughout the text. Unfortunately there is no way round "number crunching" and it is essential that you understand at least the basics. From a suite of figures it is possible to make fundamental decisions about where your business is and where it is going.

I have felt for several years that the "banks" and the "customers" are not helping each other as much as they might. This is really because an aspiring businessman is not a banker, and a banker is not a risktaker. Much of this book will be familiar to the banker (at least in cash terms) and as a result will enable you (the customer) to use the same language, thereby saving a lot of time and misunderstanding. The Co-operative Bank is to be congratulated for having the courage to sponsor this book. I would particularly like to thank Peter Walker, whose unfailing enthusiasm has not only kept me hard at it, but has successfully steered the venture through the corridors of power; Ben Palmer, who has unstintingly gone through the text and figures for me (much of it out of office hours); Editorial Services in the guise of Simon Conway, who has edited the text; and to Iain Williamson, who has brought the text to life in the form you now see it. On a more personal note my thanks are due yet again to my wife, who wrote the whole of the original text in long hand to my dictation, and to my father-in-law Bill Barnes, formerly Marketing Director to Carrington Viyella PLC, who has listened patiently to, and commented on, all my ideas over the last four and a half years.

I hope you will have as much fun running your own business as I have had getting this project off the ground. Remember, nothing can stop informed enthusiasm!

    DAVID S. PORTER

May 1988

NOTE

The Figures referred to throughout the text of this book are shown in full in the Appendices. Some Figures are reproduced in the text to help the reader.

CHAPTER ONE

YOUR OWN BOSS?

1. STARTING UP

It may be that you always felt you wanted to run your own business, but make sure you do it for the right reasons.

If you are already in employment, it is likely you made that decision because you felt you were not up to running your own business. And it could be that nothing has changed.

If you have been made redundant it really is best to exercise caution before ploughing all your money into something which either just will not work, or something which you just cannot make to work. You must be honest with yourself.

Self employment is a great alternative to the dole, but it is not the only one. Check with the bank to get advice on the best way of using your cash. Then if you DO decide to take that giant step into working for yourself, make sure that the business you choose is viable and that it will sustain you.

2. REALITIES

When you were working, let us say your annual salary was £12,500. In your own business your sales will need to be many times that amount to enable you to enjoy that same financial reward.

So just how much will it cost? Well, let us suppose that the anticipated annual expenses of running the business, excluding the purchase of stock, are £10,000. In addition to that, just to get started, you will have to buy or lease a desk or desks, cabinets, display cases, work tops, typewriters, vehicles . . . and many other items. Just how many and what kind depends, of course, on the nature of your business. So this will clearly involve you having to spend some - or maybe all - of your savings or redundancy payment.

Let us say you have £5,000 in savings or redundancy. If you simply invested that money at 10 per cent interest per annum, then it would be costing you £500 in the first year in lost interest alone.

Another potential loss is pensions. Most employers provide a pension for their employees and, as a self-employed worker, you should expect to make your own arrangements for your financial security during retirement. A reasonable amount would be £1,000 per year.

Already we can see this becoming a costly operation. The total so far looks like this:

	£	£
Cost of running the business		10,000
Lost interest on money used	500	
Your salary	12,500	
Personal Pension contribution	1,000	
		14,000
Total		£24,000

Of course, this does not include the costs of furniture and equipment mentioned earlier, nor the additional expenses incurred in employing staff or help. From these figures you can see that even if your sales, or as it is sometimes called your turnover, were to be £24,000, you would probably do better to remain in employment or, if redundant, to invest your money and go on the dole until a new opportunity presented itself.

You must aim to make a profit from your endeavour and to achieve the highest possible financial return, although you should not expect to make a profit immediately. In the longer term - and on the figures we have already used - a profit of 25 per cent on top of your expenses of £24,000 would not be unreasonable. That would mean another £6,000 a year.

3. PERSONAL SKILLS

As we have seen already, starting and running your own business always takes a great deal longer and costs a great deal more than you expect. Demands on your time are tremendous and substantial sacrifices will need to be made, so it is essential that you take into your confidence those members of your family who will be most affected by your plans. This is where your personal skills will prove most helpful, and one of the most important is being able to manage your time to best advantage. Time is at a premium. It is essential that you use it effectively.

You must be able to organise yourself AND be able to bring out the best in other people. If and when it proves necessary to employ others, you must be able to take care of them, to nurture them and develop them if you are to achieve good results. As your business grows and prospers, you may need to employ more people. More people will mean more time, but each will still need that same level of attention.

In addition to your staff, you will have to deal with suppliers, some of whom will let you down, and customers, some of whom will be unreasonable or even downright difficult.

In all this, some things will quickly become apparent: your strengths and weaknesses. You may soon discover skills which you had not originally appreciated.

4. PREFERENCES

If you are going to work for yourself, then you should enjoy yourself. Otherwise, why do it? If you do not enjoy yourself most of the time, then you are in the wrong business.

Concentrate on doing the things you are good at and delegate the rest. This will quickly identify your weaknesses and, by doing so, will enable you to bring in outside help which will assist you to expand your own expertise without affecting the growth of the business. But make no mistake: the prospect is daunting, and you need to be fit and well. You should consider the questions at the end of this chapter in order to assess your skills and capabilities.

The hardest part of starting any business is securing your first real sale, whether your business involves the sale of products or of services. A real sale must be to an independent third party in order to count. There will always be family and friends who will support you, but do not delude yourself: friends and family will not sustain a business.

5. CHOICE OF BUSINESS

How do you decide what business to go into? You may think that you could do your existing or previous job better for yourself than for your employer. This may sometimes be the case but, more often than not, it leads to difficulties.

To start with there is a tendency, particularly when your business is of a service nature, to believe that the customer is dealing with you personally. In fact of course he is merely dealing with the business as identified by you. It could be that in approaching him to see if he would come to you in the event of you leaving your company, he may well promise support. In reality, he is unlikely to leave the security of an existing business for your unproven new enterprise.

In any event the matter is more complex. First your contract of employment may well prevent you not only from carrying out a similar business, but also from dealing with existing customers of your employer. Most importantly though, you owe a duty to your present employer while you are working for him and if, during that period, you set up your own business he would quite properly object and may even start legal proceedings. But whether he did so or not, you must consider your name, your reputation and your credibility. Eventually, your business may succeed or fail on the strength of these alone. A legal case would certainly destroy all three before your business had been given a chance to stand on its own feet.

6. HOBBY OR PASTIME

Inspiration for a business venture may come from a pastime or a hobby, but objects manufactured in this way may lack the refinement necessary for a large market and they may also tend to be subjective. Just because you like a particular item or product does not necessarily mean that everyone else will. You must be realistic about a possible market. Beware particularly of collectables and items of specific minority interest.

7. EXISTING BUSINESSES

You could, of course, buy into an existing business, although it is no use entering into a business if you have no natural flair for that particular field. You might also ask yourself why the individual is selling. Is it not doing well? Or is it because of ill health, an accident, or approaching retirement? Obviously these latter three would be genuine reasons for selling or bringing in a younger or sturdier partner. But be warned: quite frequently it is because the vendors are not successful.

8. FRANCHISING

In many ways franchising is the easier route to running your own business, although it can initially be very expensive because of the goodwill or name which you are buying. There are many existing operations which allow you to use their know-how, marketing and business ideas in return for a share in your profit. Some better known examples have become household names, but the established name does not mean you do not have to work hard. Quite the opposite.

An advantage of this particular type of business venture is that you will be able to see the franchise in operation before you begin. And very often the company involved will not only provide you with all their marketing skills, but also with the necessary business information to enable a fairly trouble-free start.

The most obvious problem with a franchising operation is that even after you have started up your own operation, other people are carrying on in the same business and under the same name. This can sometimes lead to disputes if you feel fellow operators are "poaching" in your area of activity. Further, because you are part of a group - although without having any real legal or contractual obligations towards them - your own operation could be affected adversely because of the activities of someone else operating with the name under which you yourself operate.

One real benefit is undoubtedly that you can identify the risks you could be incurring by buying into the business, giving you a clear understanding of exactly what you are letting yourself in for. If you do decide to try a franchising operation, take some legal advice on the various documents you will be asked to sign - and remember that if and when you come to sell the business, the franchisor will again become involved.

9. MARKET RESEARCH

Whatever you decide to do, you will need to examine the market very carefully. In the first instance you need to decide what the national trends are likely to be. Never assume that there is an unlimited market because, in reality, markets are either rising or falling. You need to decide at what point you would be entering a cycle, and always bear in mind that your business may not be starting up immediately. So estimate the state of the markets at the time you DO start up.

Some products have longer cycles than others. For example, double-glazing has lasted a great deal longer than skate-boards, and while video shops may still have some growth in them, the original market is undoubtedly over-serviced.

You need to consider the national influences which will affect your proposals. In this context you should not only read the trade magazines and newspapers relevant to your business, but also an established financial journal such as the *Financial Times*. The *Financial Times* is, of course, indispensable for large businesses, but you will be surprised how frequently the actions of major companies will both affect and mirror the situation in your own business. For example, you may discover from its pages that one of your customers or suppliers has become the target of a takeover. Always retain an open and inquiring mind.

(i) The local environment

Having considered the national situation, you then need to think about the local position. If you are opening a shop, it is clearly sensible to investigate the life expectancy of the existing housing of the community which you intend to serve. If housing is scheduled for demolition then check whether new housing is planned. Also, you must consider the similar businesses in your area - the competition! - and make assessments of their strengths and weaknesses.

(ii) Target market

By this time you should have narrowed down the market you wish to serve. What you are trying to do is find a gap in the market . . . a gap which is not being serviced.

On a grand scale, for example, the Japanese saw an opening for the small and portable television, and exploited it to considerable advantage. But, quite often, good business ideas involve a large amount of luck in their success stories and, frequently, in trying to satisfy one particular market, another is inadvertently opened. The replacement of electric typewriters, for example, was achieved by selling computers with word-processor packages. In this way, computers effectively became typewriters.

Your target market relates specifically to the business you have in mind. If you are contemplating manufacturing, then it will be necessary to have made samples of the product which can be shown to your potential customers. By this method you could establish interest in your product, and even conceivably secure some orders, before actually starting large scale production - and before running up the huge costs involved.

A great deal of time and effort is required to build up a demand for your product or service. You must get it as close to perfection in the first instance as you can. You will, of course, be constantly refining and improving both your product and your techniques for its production, and you can only learn from experience.

All great business ventures and endeavours started from just an idea. Put YOUR idea to the bank, which will give you an objective view, and will undoubtedly highlight those areas that may need more thought.

10. RISK

Before leaving this chapter, spare a moment to consider the risks involved. In the initial enthusiasm of an idea, the enormity and the consequences of what you could be taking on may not be fully appreciated.

When you run your own business, the buck stops with you! If you get it wrong, it might mean no more than a dent to your ego. But it could also mean the loss of your house, your savings, and your family! Identify all areas of risk properly, and plan accordingly.

11. INFORMATION THE BANK WILL REQUIRE

(i) The names and addresses of those contemplating the venture.
(ii) Present wages or salaries - if redundant, then wage or salary while in employment.
(iii) Did employment include a pension?
(iv) Cash savings and investments currently available. What portion will be put into the new business?
(v) Can you organise other people?
(vi) Have you suffered any illness within the last five years?
(vii) What product or service do you have in mind, and what experience have you had in this area?
(viii) What competition is there within the locality?
(ix) Who are your likely clients or customers?

CHAPTER TWO

STRUCTURE OF THE BUSINESS

1. INTRODUCTION

How do you structure a business? There are many ways and many different forms, and some are more suited than others to a particular type of business. Whether you operate as a sole trader, a partnership or a limited company, there are different factors which can affect the way your business behaves. In the case of a sole trader or a partnership, it is the individual proprietors who are the people who run the business, and consequently they take all the risk. In general terms, risks might include the following:

(i) Financial liability

This means, basically, that the proprietor will be personally responsible for all financial liability however it might arise. This includes all the expenses, and is irrespective of the business's level of profitability.

(ii) Product or service liability

Although many business activities are unlikely to involve the proprietor in any risk - clothes pegs, plastic cups, etc. - many products and services can involve very high risk, particularly if they have a technical involvement. Structural engineering, aircraft manufacture, medicine and the law are obvious examples of high risk. Many of the professions are still able to obtain insurance for professional negligence, and your bank can help to place such an insurance, even where the professional body organises its own cover. For example, indemnity for lawyers should be extended to cover more than the basic risks. We all recognise, however, that insurance itself will not cover all circumstances and it is for this reason that the limited liability company is used.

2. SOLE TRADER

You may well start in business on your own. If you do, at least you have the satisfaction of knowing that any success you might have is yours and yours alone. Further, any money you make will not have to be shared with anyone - but remember not to spend it all as there will be bills to pay! If your risks are to be high, then you might decide to share the risk with a partner or form a limited company.

As a sole trader the risks are threefold:

(i) You will have to pay all the expenses of the business, whether or not you are making any money.
(ii) Income tax will be payable on all your profits, if you make any. The times of payment are discussed later in the book.
(iii) If you do the work negligently you will be personally liable, and if your customer sues you successfully, he or she can look to you and all your assets to reimburse the loss.

You may well feel that you would like to be involved with a partner or form a limited company.

3. PARTNERSHIP

"A trouble shared is a trouble halved," they say, and of course it is possible to share the risk with others. In some situations, however, it is not permitted to form a limited liability company, and it makes good sense in those situations not only to insure your liability, but to share the business so that individual expertise can be harnessed to the full. It can be very comforting to operate within a partnership, enabling you to ask others for their views on running the business. It also allows for certain degrees of specialisation.

Remember, though, that while an individual is liable for his own actions or mistakes, partners are usually jointly and severally liable. This means that you will not only be liable for your own actions and mistakes, but also for those of your partner or partners. If, for example, any of your partners fail to pay their income tax, you may have to pay it for them - how you get it back from them is YOUR problem, of course. Start as you mean to continue: organise a formal partnership document setting out the terms of the agreement between each of you, which will be particularly helpful when the business expands.

If you fail to do this, the Partnership Act of 1890 states in broad terms that where two or more people run an enterprise with a view to profit, they share the profits and liabilities equally, unless there is a contrary intention. This may well arise where partners have contributed capital disproportionately.

4. LIMITED LIABILITY COMPANY

Whether you should form a company should, in the first instance, depend on the risk for which you think you are liable. As the business expands the financial exposure also increases, and if this is likely to reach unacceptable levels then limited liability should be sought. Similarly, where the activity could give rise to product liability, a company should be formed. A company can be bought off the shelf for less than £300 and tailored to your needs.

A company is of course a legal entity in its own right, and can enter into contractural relationships in much the same way as can a private individual or partner. The liability of the shareholders (ie. the proprietors) is limited to the value of the company. If the company falls on hard times, the shareholders will usually lose only their shares, not their possessions or other assets.

Where you operate through a company, it is not uncommon for third parties - the most usual being landlords, suppliers and banks - to require personal guarantees from the shareholders and directors. If you are asked to sign such a guarantee, you should understand exactly what is happening. Basically, the person doing business with you is asking you personally to underwrite the risk. If three of you are borrowing £30,000 from the bank, then you may well be asked not only to find £10,000 but the full £30,000. This is because, as you will recall, your liability is to be joint and several. In such a situation you should ask yourself where the money will come from if you have to pay off the guarantee. If the answer involves actually selling your home, you should ask yourself if that is something you really want to have to do. Probably not, but if you want to run your own business alone, or in partnership, then you may have to. Think it through so you will be aware of the risks.

The insolvency legislation has introduced penalties with regard to the operation of a company which the directors know to be in financial difficulties. The subject is too complex to be dealt with here, but obviously the legislation makes officers in limited companies much more accountable. It no longer pays to be cavalier about running a company.

Similarly, unless the business has a realistic value in the event of an enforced sale, the bank may well require the security of the home or homes of the proprietor/s. If your home is going to be used as security, then you will have to discuss the matter with your immediate family or certainly those for whom your home IS a home. The law is rightly anxious to look after your family, particularly where their home is concerned, and your bank will need to be satisfied that everyone involved fully understands the situation. To this end, the bank will require that they are separately advised when the appropriate charge is signed. Remember, guarantees and loans have a habit of needing repayment when you are least able to meet the expense. Do not let your enthusiasm - though essential if you are to succeed! - overcome your common sense. Do not ignore the risks you may be taking for yourself and your family.

5. WORKERS' CO-OPERATIVE

Another structure you may wish to consider is the workers' co-operative. This is a business owned and democratically run by the members who are mainly or entirely employees of the firm. Co-operatives are different from other types of business because their operating principles are different. These are:

- Membership is open to all employees.
- Members have equal voting rights: one member one vote, irrespective of their financial involvement.

- The return on any investment in the co-operative is limited to a reasonable rate.
- Any profits are distributed according to work put in, not according to money invested.

Many people claim that one of the major benefits of co-operative businesses is increased job satisfaction for the employees. A number of standard companies have seen the benefits and are now introducing profit sharing schemes for their employees.

Other benefits might be a low level of conflict because owners and workers are one and the same; and high quality products and services because of increased motivation and a greater awareness of business realities among employees due to their involvement in the running of the business. After all, if your employees knew your business was having cash flow problems, they would be less likely to ask for wage increases.

Co-operatives DO require dedication and commitment. Members must be prepared to take on extra responsibilities and to participate in the running of the business. Most co-operatives elect to register as a corporate body with limited liability, either through incorporation under the Companies Act or by registration under the Industrial & Provident Societies Acts.

6. QUESTIONS YOU MUST ASK YOURSELF

Unless you are happy to set up and run your business as a sole trader, with all the risks that involves, you should certainly consider one of the other options discussed above. In making a decision, these points must be taken into account:

(i) What is to be the name of the business, and does it conflict with any other?
(ii) If you have partners, how long do you expect to stay together?
(iii) Have you some premises to operate from? If you are starting from your own home or that of your partner, will allowance be made for overhead expenses to be paid to that partner?

(iv) Can you legally operate from home? Do you need planning or building regulation permission and/or is there a covenant in the title to prevent you from operating from home (this may also be true of ANY property that you might choose to use)?

(v) Are you all injecting the same amount of cash, or is one of you contributing only expertise?

(vi) Are you sharing the profits equally, or is there to be a salary paid to the working partner before the profits are divided?

(vii) If the profits are to be shared unequally, will the liabilities be shared on the same basis?

(viii) Who are to be your accountants? Avoid using a friend who will do it in his spare time: this creates more problems than it solves.

(ix) Have you decided on your banking requirements and filled in the appropriate forms?

(x) What insurance cover is required - life, sickness, or professional and public liability?

(xi) How many days annual holiday will you be taking?

(xii) Will any of the partners be able to pursue other business interests outside that of the partnership?

(xiii) Has retirement of any partner been considered? On what basis can a partner be expelled?

(xiv) If a partner dies, will the partnership be dissolved or must the other partners buy him or her out? If the latter, then at what price, and who decides if you cannot agree - the accountant or an independent third party?

(xv) What restrictions, if any, are to be incorporated in the deed to prevent a retiring partner starting up in competition with the existing business? Make sure the proposals are reasonable otherwise they will not be enforceable.

CHAPTER THREE

HOW TO MAKE A PROFIT

1. PROPOSALS

By now, you will probably have spent quite a bit of time just thinking about starting a business. And if you are running one already, now is probably a good time to step back and take a good look at your current position. Either way, you must actually understand the type of business which you have chosen for yourself.

The financial considerations which you must take into account will be the same, at least in general terms, no matter what you do. But if you do not have a fundamental understanding of your product AND your market place, then you may never succeed. Companies which have already achieved success often turn their attention to areas which have no connection with their original service or the original skills with which the company was created. Needless to say, this rarely - if ever - pays off.

2. INFORMATION

In both new and existing businesses, information gathering is crucial. The more information the better. You cannot know too much about your business.

Business is about risk; we told you that in Chapter One. But you can minimise that risk simply by making sure you understand the ins and outs of your particular field and its operation. It is important, for example, to know not only what your gross turnover will be, but also how it is made up. Each existing or potential area of activity in your business must be specifically identified so that you know its effects on - and contributions to - your turnover. Do not forget: looking after the turnover will itself look after the profits. If a single part of your business is not making profit, you need to know.

At the same time, you must identify the expenses of your operation - not just in general terms, but in specific relation to individual areas. In this way you will soon identify the true cost of the operation.

With the turnover and expenses known, the net profit is identifiable. And when you relate that net profit to your turnover, you will be able to work out as a percentage the actual profit margin. If your expenses remain constant but your turnover rises then, clearly, your profit margin will be bigger. You will make more money. But if, because of some lack of control, your turnover stays the same while your costs increase, then your profit drops. The margin is, basically, what you keep, and it can be a difficult concept to grasp.

From this you see that the aim of any business should be to hold costs and expenses down to an absolute minimum while maintaining output or production at an absolute maximum - always remembering, of course, to ensure that the quality remains the same throughout.

Always be careful to obtain the right kind of business. An approach from a substantial and well-known firm should be examined with great care. Do not convince yourself it is merely because you are absolutely brilliant. Equally, do not think for a minute that the firm is giving you a good start. In business, people really do look after themselves.

Ask yourself instead, why have I been approached? If you cannot understand the firm's motives, then ask them. And while you are doing so, suggest that, because you have not been running your business for too long, they might be prepared to pay at least for raw materials in advance. You might as well find out at the beginning just what the realities of business are rather than completing the work and then having to wait seemingly endlessly for payment.

3. THE SHAPE YOU ARE IN

When you are planning your business for the first time, you will have very little to go on in the way of past experience. If, however, you have decided on what your turnover needs to be for your business to be viable, you will have found a good starting point.

In an existing business, your profit and loss account will contain both your gross turnover and your expenses. Accounts are just information in figure form. You must have those figures constantly at hand in order to give yourself every chance of making the right decisions. Make your figures guide your planning and forecasting and prepare accounts regularly.

(i) Expenses

When you set up your business there will be some one-off costs, such as legal fees, valuation fees, promotional costs and so on. Because of these one-offs, your profitability will be distorted - the profit margin narrower - during your first year. After that, expenses will settle down.

In an existing business, the profit and loss account prepared by your accountant will list all expenses, usually in no particular order of significance. These will fall into two collective categories: fixed expenses and overheads; and variable expenses.

Fixed expenses represent wages, while overheads relate to costs incurred simply because you are in business. These include rent, rates, gas, electricity and so on. Variable expenses are more or less everything else and are usually far more controllable. They will usually include advertising, marketing, entertaining, telephone and such like. It is the controllability of these expenses, giving the opportunity for a bit of fine tuning, which can improve profitability. In Chapter Four these costs will be discussed in greater detail to show the profitability of different areas.

(ii) Margin

To make profit, you must first bring in enough money to cover your expenses. When you have done that, the rest IS profit. And the difference between the two is your margin. The whole shape of your business will be shown simply by deducting your expenses from your turnover. Remember this: it is far easier to control margins by reducing costs than it is by increasing sales.

4. IDENTIFYING YOUR EXPENSES

In this section we consider two sets of accounts, one relating to a service industry, the other to the manufacturing and retail industries.

While a complete set of figures for each is contained in the Appendices, some parts of those figures are included in the text. You should refer to the appropriate set for your type of business (starting with Figures 1 and 12) if you wish to consider them in detail. For simplicity it is assumed that the figures will be the same for a new business as for a going concern. As we have already suggested, figures in a new business will most probably show higher expenses (due to setting up costs) and lower turnover in the first year, but after the first year they should improve and bear some resemblance to those used in the example. In either case the principles are the same. You need to examine carefully your likely expenses.

(i) Wages

(a) Wages

These relate to all the employees of the business. You should check the individual wages paid or to be paid, first to ensure that there is no imbalance which might lead to difficulties in the future, and secondly to see if they may be redistributed, for example, by job-sharing or part-time work.

(b) Drawings

This is the amount the proprietors hope to take out of the business.

If you are assessing a true profit you should bear in mind that while you would actually get paid if you were working for somebody else, in a relatively new business the proprietors may well not be able regularly to draw very much for themselves. Initially they may have to rely on the occasional drawings, and only then when the opportunities present themselves. In other words, when funds are available. This is principally because such funds that are generated are needed to keep the business going, although additional money can be withdrawn if the profitability and cash available will allow. See Chapter Six on cash flow.

(ii) Office expenses

(a) Books

In a service industry it may be necessary to keep up-to-date, and books can represent an expensive commodity. There should be a consistent buying policy, and the up-dates need checking carefully. Perhaps a criterion would be: are they being read and providing new ideas?

(b) Photo-copying/printing/stationery

The quality of these items is clearly dependent on the nature of your business. This must relate to your marketing strategy (which is discussed elsewhere) but as a general rule you should shop around.

(c) Cars and typewriters

Whether these items are included as an office expense, and accordingly highlighted, or placed under miscellaneous, will depend on their relative importance in the business. In a professional practice such as a lawyer or accountant they may be fundamental to style, whereas in a manufacturing business they may only be a necessary evil. It is for you to decide, but having made your decision you should be consistent. All the items which appear in the figures are, to a certain extent, arbitrary. But in trying to assess the shape of your business, it is important that you can justify all items of expenditure.

(d) Vehicles

In a manufacturing or retail business vehicles will be needed to move stock and finished goods. Again you should think about costs and maximise vehicle use, perhaps by use of trailers, for instance.

(iii) Premises expenses

(a) Rent
Your potential premises and the terms of the lease should be examined to decide whether they will be adequate, both in the short and medium terms. You will need to know whether the layout is correct and suitable for your present business and its growth. If this is the case, the rent or mortgage repayment will be a necessary expense.

(b) Rates
The building you are operating from will again dictate this amount, but spreading the payments on a monthly basis might be helpful.

(c) Electricity and gas
The installations should be checked periodically to ensure that there is no wastage. Assess the effective use of your electricity or gas supply, and if this represents a significant part of your expenditure, then the availability of a grant should be investigated.

(iv) Finance
The headings here are self-evident but both bank charges and loan interest will be dependent on your future plans. As far as the accountants are concerned, it may be possible for payment to be made on a monthly basis. In any event, fees can be negotiated.

(a) Insurance
Many of the risks that you might incur can be easily identified and insured against, but the problem with all types of insurance is knowing the level at which to obtain cover. This is a fairly specialised area and the bank will always be able to advise you accordingly.

Basically, you need to protect the assets required to run your business. General insurance cover is available for such things as fire and theft, but it is also necessary to insure your vehicles and probably your goods while they are in transit.

Most insurance cover can be obtained on an all-risks basis, which means that you do not lose out when you make a claim. However, if you can improve the internal organisation of your business so as to reduce the risks involved, then you might well reduce the cost of the insurance cover.

The installation of a burglar alarm or sprinkler system, for example, usually brings the rates down. Similarly, the age of any drivers you employ might well affect the rates of insurance cover premiums and excesses of your vehicles.

Once you have considered the assets of the business you ought to think about the earnings it is going to generate. If the business burns down, or you are ill, the money could stop coming in. But these are not the only potential pitfalls. It is not uncommon for a substantial business to go into liquidation, and if this unhappy event overtook several of your customers, or even one large one, it could have a severe effect on your cash flow. Credit insurance is available to protect against this but, again, it is a matter of deciding how much cover you want.

In spite of the above, there may be some cover that you simply cannot do without. Apart from covering your liability to your employees (which is compulsory), you should also arrange insurance cover against third party liability. This relates to injury or damage to a customer or any other individual arising from your operation. An example may be somebody falling over one of your products which has been left lying around, thus causing themselves injury. Result: they could sue you for negligence.

But the real risk in your business will relate to the service you are giving, or the product you are selling . . . or both! As more and more people become involved in businesses, and the business environment becomes more complicated, it gets harder to obtain insurance of this type. And this is why many businesses form limited liability companies.

One obvious form of insurance is on your own life. Running your own business creates strain, which can lead to illness, and insurance taken out on yourself should at least cover death. Other insurances can protect your income should you become too ill to work, with payments starting after an agreed period of sickness or disability.

Then, of course, you should consider your retirement. In fact, one of the main problems of running your own business is that you have to arrange your own pension. Even though the Government allows you to spend a proportion of your income (allowable against tax) on pension premiums, it is not always easy or convenient to save sufficient out of your cash flow in order to produce a pension similar to what you might enjoy if you were in employment. After all, most employed people - certainly those at managerial level - would hope to achieve a pension equivalent to two thirds of their income at retirement. Starting to provide for a pension becomes more expensive as you get older simply because you have less time in which to save. It might be worth entering into a small commitment right at the beginning, if only to create the habit, and thus underline the point that not ALL your profit can go into your pocket.

(b) Depreciation

Machinery and plant will require replacement over a period of time and the amount you need to spend will undoubtedly be more than the original cost. In order to reflect the true worth of your assets, it is usual to reduce their value to nil during the course of their useful life. For example, if a machine has a value when new of £1,000 and will last five years, then £200 will be deducted each year. But you must remember that this is only a book entry and will not represent a cash saving - unless you create a fund out of which the new replacement machine will eventually be purchased.

If you have surplus funds, or you wish to set up an appropriate account, the bank will advise you which is the best way of going about it. Frequently there is insufficient cash at the beginning to save anything, but if depreciation is not included, you may be deluding yourself as to your true profits.

(v) Miscellaneous and sundries

In many ways this will probably be the area which needs most thought. There is a tendency to debit this account without actually giving much thought to the expenditure entailed - and thus the cumulative amount over the year can become excessive. It is advisable to keep a close eye on this particular cost and examine it with some care. The accounts from the service industry (Figure 1) have been itemised in detail to show some of the more common areas of expense.

FIGURE 1: PROFIT & LOSS ACCOUNT

	Year 1 £		Year 2 £	% turnover
Income	43322	Fees (see Fig 2)	46787	100
Wages	16509	Wages	17500	
	4750	Drawings	5000	
	21259	Total	22500	48
Office Expenses	532	Books	564	
	2115	Photocopying	472	
	928	Postages	984	
	1260	Telephone	1336	
	641	Stationery	680	
	1698	Cars	1800	
	450	Typewriters	500	
	7624	Total	6336	14
Building Expenses	2750	Rent	2750	
	583	Rates	688	
	162	Electricity	176	
	120	Gas	130	
	296	Repairs	320	
	3911	Total	4064	9
Finance	266	Bank Interest	350	
	10	Donations	15	
	245	Insurance	275	
	650	Auditors	750	
	1075	Advertising	1150	
	1328	Depreciation	1395	
	3574	Total	3935	8
Miscellaneous	75	Courses	85	
	300	Entertainment	225	
	228	Parking	300	
	500	Staff Adverts	360	
	85	Newspapers	125	
	1637	Sundries	1965	
	2825	Total	3060	6
	39193	TOTAL EXPENSES	39895	85
	4129	PROFIT BEFORE TAX	6892	15

(vi) Stock

The level of stock that a business needs to carry is, to a certain extent, a matter of trial and error. But remember that you will not want to turn customers away regularly because you have run out of what they need. In a manufacturing industry you undoubtedly require raw materials and finished goods.

(a) Raw materials

The amount of raw materials you have on hand depends on your product; the length of time it takes to make the finished article; the volume of finished stock you need to hold in order to accommodate sales; and the scarcity of supply of your raw materials - in other words, how difficult is it to get hold of if you should run out? All this could total up to six weeks supply of raw materials, four weeks in production and a further six to eight weeks of finished stock.

(b) Finished goods

Depending entirely upon the nature of your business, the stock level of finished goods could fluctuate wildly.

In a retail business you will, of course, not have to consider raw materials, but only the finished goods, many of which will have different levels of stock for fairly obvious reasons. In a television and hi-fi store, for example, you will obviously carry more batteries than TVs.

Different stocks will be sold at different speeds, but you will quickly become aware of the various requirements. In a manufacturing business, finished goods will represent completed stock which, as in a retail business, has yet to be sold. In each case a constant check is necessary, with slow moving items being cleared at sale times. Most personal computers can now be easily programmed to deal with stock control. If you are familiar with the use of computers, you should seriously consider using them.

(c) Stock turn

It should be absolutely clear that, because stock is NOT cash, stock LEVELS are critical to cash flow, and you should try to manage on as little as possible without actually damaging your sales potential. If you can persuade your supplier either to fund part of the stock or to give you credit, so much the better. In the "cut, make and trim" industry, for example, this is a well accepted procedure in that your customers usually provide the cloth for you to "make up" at their own expense.

If you decide to change the nature of your business, this may fundamentally change the shape of your concern, which could be disastrous. For example, if a "cut, make and trim" factory decided to produce their own line, they would suddenly discover that they were not only funding higher stock levels, but also carrying the risk of it being the wrong stock. The bank can help you with the financing of your stock and can advise accordingly. Details are set out in Chapter Seven.

(d) Mathematics

You can calculate how often you turn over your stock in one year, but you must appreciate that this calculation does not identify which element of stock is moving, only what is happening on average.

Extract from Figure 12

	Year 1 £			Year 2 £	%T/over	% G. Profit
Sales	101322	Sales (see Fig 13)		112287	100	
Materials	10000	Opening stock	14000			
	62000	Add Purchases	69000			
	72000	Total	83000			
	14000	Less Closing Stock	17500			
	58000	Cost of Sales		65500		
	43322	Gross Profit		46787	42	100

In a manufacturing business, stock not only includes raw materials purchased, but also reflects work actually in progress and levels of finished stock. In Figure 12 you can see that the opening stock was £14,000 and the closing stock is £17,500, giving an average of £15,750. This figure is then divided into the figure for purchases for that year (£69,000) giving just over four.

This means in that twelve-month period, you turned your stock over four times. Whether this is sufficient depends on your type of business. If you are selling food, then clearly it is not, but it may well be if you are building sailing yachts.

(vii) Conclusion

If you have never thought of breaking down your expenses in this way before, then you have learned a very valuable lesson. By this method you will undoubtedly highlight items which will surprise you. In a new business it will assist in realising all the areas of expenditure you need to think about, thus enabling you to control them more accurately in the future. When comparing figures over the years, however, the effects of inflation must be taken into account.

Expenses, as incurred, should be recorded under specific headings. Most book keeping systems have a provision to carry out individual figures to an analysis column which not only makes it easy to add up at the end of each page and each month, but also helps to identify the total expense in each category. These can then be used for comparison against your forecast.

5. TURNOVER

As your business grows in size and becomes more successful, you will undoubtedly become more detached from the day to day running of it. You may tend to be involved with more important matters and, as a result, your over-view of the business could become distorted. In handling the more important customers you may forget what your basic business is about. It is unlikely that mere accounts will reveal the contribution made to your turnover by the individual products or services you sell. Two things to remember from figures are that value added tax is not normally included and your turnover figure will not represent cash receipts - but this is discussed in more detail in Chapter Six.

It is essential that you identify the principal areas of activity and, by so doing, reveal your product mix. These have been identified alphabetically as A - O in Figures 2 and 13 which set out the likely breakdown.

Prepare a sheet with the departments (1 - 5) identified on the left hand side and the product or service (A - O) along the top. Record the arrival of the product AND the department to which it goes by the simple means of placing a tick in the appropriate line/column. At the end of each month you simply convert the ticks to numbers and thus identify very accurately the type of business you are handling. You can use the same system for invoices as well as incoming business and your business plan should refer to this product

New

	A	B	C	D	E	F	G	H	I	J	K	L	M	N	O	Totals
Department 1	✓✓	✓✓✓✓✓			✓✓✓											0
Department 2	✓	✓✓✓✓	✓✓✓	✓✓	✓✓											0
Department 3						✓✓	✓	✓✓✓✓	✓✓✓							0
Department 4		✓				✓✓✓	✓✓	✓✓✓	✓✓✓✓	✓✓✓✓	✓✓	✓	✓			0
Department 5										✓	✓✓✓	✓	✓		✓✓✓	0
Totals	0	0	0	0	0	0	0	0	0	0	0	0	0	0	0	0

Invoiced

	A	B	C	D	E	F	G	H	I	J	K	L	M	N	O	Totals
Department 1	2	8			5											15
Department 2	1	5	3	2	2											13
Department 3						2	1	4	7							14
Department 4		1				3	2	3	4	8	2	1	1			25
Department 5										1	3	1	1		4	10
Totals	3	13	4	2	7	5	3	7	11	9	5	2	2	0	4	77

mix when you are considering future expansion. The bank can assist in preparing appropriate figures and draft business plans and forecasts are contained in the Appendices.

Breakdown of turnover

If you have been in business some time or are starting a new business you will obviously be aware of your principal activity. All businesses have a "core" element and peripheral activities. You should therefore isolate, on paper, your principal line from your other areas of activity.

For example, if you are in the paint manufacturing business, your own paint lines will probably represent the major part of your business unless you are manufacturing for a DIY chain or some other big organisation. You will probably manufacture different types of paint, and indeed various painting and decorating related products, but the actual manufacturing of paint will be your main business. If you are a butcher you may specialise in one type of meat in preference to others: beef may be your major line with lamb and chicken as secondary.

What is true of all businesses is that their principal activities may well represent 75 per cent of the total turnover. The remaining 25 per cent may well have to be identified in part as miscellaneous. If 75 per cent of your customers account for the bulk of your business, then it makes sense to spend your time in thinking of ways and means by which this area could be improved and made even MORE profitable. Using that valuable time in areas which produce far less return is obviously not sensible.

If you have not previously identified your turnover, it will be necessary to go through all your invoices and divide them physically into the particular ranges you have already decided. In doing this, you may well discover that some activities are playing a larger part than you thought. From Figures 2 and 13 you will see that the core groups 1 and 2 account for 75 per cent of the business.

FIGURE 2: ANALYSIS OF TURNOVER

	Product	Amount Invoiced £	Core Total £	%
Core Group 1	A	4610		
	B	6442		
	C	3608		
	D	1980		
	E	2075	18715	40
Core Group 2	F	7298		
	G	3270		
	H	2806		
	I	3000	16374	35
Core Group 3	J	3808		
	K	1483		
	L	791	6082	13
Core Group 4	M	3167		
	N	882	4049	9
Miscellaneous	O	1567	1567	3
TOTAL			46787	100

The groups have been sub-divided, with each sub-division represented by a letter. How many sub-divisions you have is entirely dependent on the type of business you are in, although they should represent sufficiently large parts of your business to be useful for comparison. When you have decided on the particular headings, you should add up the separate invoices or bills in each heading. In this way you will know the volume of activity.

Let us say, for example, that the group A figure (£4,610) represents 100 items. This would give an average price per item of £46.10. The group B figure (£6,442) represents 1,000 items giving an average price per item of £6.44. Now, by taking into account the expenses incurred in each department, you can show actual profit figures. As a result you may try to increase sales in the group that shows a higher profit per item figure.

This is a rather simplistic example, but it is not uncommon to discover with this sort of analysis that there are areas of your business which could well bear some careful thought and reorganisation. It might even be that you should finish one line altogether if you find it is not making enough profit or, indeed, is actually losing money. Finishing a line could release labour, machinery or capital for use on your more profitable work. Instead of the turnover being reduced, it might even be improved with the added bonus of a higher margin.

6. FUTURE RECORDS

Clearly it is not practical to split the invoices this way at the end of each year. It would be preferable, having decided on the individual groupings, to record them as the work comes in. Depending on the size of your business, this can either be done manually or by computer. If you decide against a computer, at least initially, then you will have to analyse the figures in book keeping ledgers.

If you use letters for each type of product within your core groups, you will be able to head up each column accordingly. During the month you will record each new order under the appropriate section and, at the end of the month, add up the invoices or bills sent out in each group to give the *value* of business, and add up the individual entries to give you the *volume*.

As far as new work is concerned you can analyse the orders when they arrive, both in terms of number and value. If you prepare the form as set out in Figure 2, you can record the new business orders as placed. You could also use the same format to record the details of the number of jobs invoiced. In this way you could assess whether the work was moving through quickly enough. If not, you could identify where the delay is occurring and do something about it. This will be very helpful when forward planning. As a result of these records you can avoid being taken by surprise if the market place changes from time to time. You will also know whether you are keeping in line with your projections and, if not, you should know why and be able to take adequate steps.

Having reached this point, you will have a full detail of your expenses, turnover and profit for the year. In the examples from Figure 1, we see a profit margin of 15 per cent.

Extract from Figure 1

	Year 1 £		Year 2 £	% turnover
	1075	Advertising	1150	
	1328	Depreciation	1395	
	3574	Total	3935	8
Miscellaneous	75	Courses	85	
	300	Entertainment	225	
	228	Parking	300	
	500	Staff Adverts	360	
	85	Newspapers	125	
	1637	Sundries	1965	
	2825	Total	3060	6
	39193	TOTAL EXPENSES	39895	85
	4129	PROFIT BEFORE TAX	6892	15

This may not be what you expected, and if not then you need to take some action. If you do nothing, the shape will get progressively worse. Unfortunately, standing still is not an option which is open to you. Assuming for the present that the shape is right, then you can with some confidence make an educated guess about next year's activity and, in general terms, about the direction you think the business should take.

7. INFORMATION THE BANK WILL REQUIRE

(i) Details of your guess of your likely turnover and expenses for your first year or details of your most recent profit and loss account.

(ii) Details of how your books are kept (manually or by computer).

(iii) The name and address of:

>Your solicitor
>Your accountant.

Plus the names of specific contacts within those firms.

CHAPTER FOUR

FORECASTS AND BUDGETS

1. THE BUSINESS PLAN

(i) Introduction

Having established the "figures" for your business in Chapter Three, it is now possible to make a plan for the future. If you are just starting out in business you will have made these assumptions already and forecasting as described in this Chapter will only apply to subsequent years. If you have been running for a year or more, your accountant will have given you year end figures as a base from which to operate.

Forecasting and budgeting have been successfully used by many businesses and are simply extensions of your first year estimates - but now you have the added benefit of at least one year of your business actually under your belt.

All too frequently some business people claim that their enterprise is peculiar. "It's not possible to make assumptions for the future," they say. Of course, this is just not true. It has already been established that your business is likely to behave in much the same way as in previous years - who knows, it might even prosper without any apparent help from yourself! But it really is essential to have some idea of your future plans. Bear in mind, though, that occasionally even your best estimate will be wrong, but if you compare what actually happens with what you thought would happen, you may well be able to put yourself back on course.

(ii) Background

Everyone knows that time is at a premium. There are often simply too few hours in the day. But time properly spent, with the bank's help, may in the longer term save you money. For example, if you have tried to collate your figures as suggested in Chapter One, then you will already have used up several hours. It is not time wasted, of course, but because of the constraints on your time, you may not be keeping up with the economy in general. There is no substitute for an hour spent reading the financial press and the various trade journals relevant to your business.

It should have been no surprise to architects, for instance, that parts of their business were on the decline during the mid-1980's because of the lower level of new building activity. Many were surprised though and, having gone on a shorter week, blamed the economy, the Government or conditions generally.

As you are responsible for your own business, you owe it to yourself, your family and to those who work for you to try to read the signs . . . look ahead. Being alive to the general business environment is a great help.

(iii) Comparisons

It does not matter what type of business you are in, nor what size - limited company, co-operative, partnership or sole trader - the bank can assist you as far as your corporate competitors are concerned. The bank can and will inquire on your behalf to the Registrar of Companies, as to the financial condition of those limited companies in competition with you. All limited companies must file returns and, while these are not complete, they should provide a very good understanding of what your competitors are doing. Of course, you may rest assured that the opposite applies also, and if you are a limited company, then your competitors will also know all about you. Remember too that your own sales force will be in constant contact with other sales people within the same industry, which may or may not assist.

For other areas of business such as the "professions" there are various inter-firm comparisons. Again, the bank can assist you in contacting them so that you can compare your own results with those of others in the same market place. There is really no excuse, in the context of the general environment, for being unaware of exactly what is happening.

2. BUDGETING EXPENSES

Even if you feel that you cannot realistically estimate your turnover, you must ensure that you know exactly what your expenses are AND that you can quantify them. If inflation is running at, say, 5 per cent it would be naive to expect that

FIGURE 3: FORECAST OF EXPENSES

		Last Year £	% Rise	Forecast £
Income	Fees (see Fig 2)	46787	11	51934
Wages	Wages	17500	9	19075
	Drawings	5000	9	5450
	Total......................	22500	9	24525
Office	Books	564	5	592
Expenses	Photocopying	472	5	496
	Postages	984	5	1033
	Telephone	1336	5	1403
	Stationery	680	5	714
	Cars	1800	5	1890
	Typewriters	500	5	525
	Total......................	6336	5	6653
Building	Rent	2750	0	2750
Expenses	Rates	688	5	722
	Electricity	176	5	185
	Gas	130	5	137
	Repairs	320	5	336
	Total......................	4064		4130
Finance	Bank Interest	350	5	368
	Donations	15	5	16
	Insurance	275	5	289
	Auditors	750	5	788
	Advertising	1150	5	1208
	Depreciation	1395	–	1465
	Total......................	3935	5	4134
Misc.	Course	85	5	89
	Entertainment	225	5	236
	Sundries	2750	5	2888
	Total......................	3060	5	3213
	TOTAL EXPENSES	39895		42655
	PROFIT BEFORE TAX	6892		9279

your expenses will not increase by at least that amount. Why "at least"? If you feel that your expenses are increasing faster than inflation, it may be that you are incurring more expenses rather than simply paying a higher figure for the same amount. Clearly, if this is happening, a cost-cutting exercise should be comparatively easy to achieve.

The next chapter will deal with actually analysing your results, but you will be comparing your forecasts with your actual results, at least monthly, and if your assumptions are wrong then you will have to reconsider the position. Using figures from the previous year, it is possible to forecast the likely expenses for the following year (see Figures 3 and 14). Figure 14 relates to a manufacturing and retail business. The general comments cover both sets of figures, but there are specific differences which will be dealt with in the text.

3. SERVICE INDUSTRY

Now that you have identified specific areas of expenditure, and you have the figures of the preceeding year as well, it should not be too difficult to make an accurate estimate for the current year.

(i) Wages

Figure 3 assumes that you do have previous figures against which you can calculate outgoings for the next year. If you are starting for the first time you will not yet have arrived at this position. But you will have to do it for the following year, so it may be no bad thing to have a go now.

You will have a good idea of the specific wages in your own industry. You should already have examined your wages carefully and have identified ways of cost-cutting and saving in some areas, but an increase of around 3 per cent above inflation might, realistically, be what you can expect. If you believe it should be a lesser figure, then you should use it. Be careful though that you always remember to include inflation.

(ii) Office expenses
(a) Books

As a result of earlier considerations you have decided that

your level of expenditure for books was too high last year and so a 5 per cent increase would be enough.

(b) Photo-copying

Again, you have inquired of various suppliers and discovered that you can replace your existing machinery at less cost.

(c) Postage

Big inroads have been made into the Post Office monopoly and there are several private firms who are quoting figures with savings of more than a third on ordinary Post Office rates. As you are expecting more business next year, an increase of 5 per cent may be viable.

It is not necessary to go through all the figures, but you will see from Figure 3 that a proposed increase on the office expenses from £6,336 to £6,653 is anticipated. This gives a monthly figure of £554, and represents 16 per cent of your total expenditure.

Extract from Figure 3

		Last Year £	% Rise	Forecast £
Office	Books	564	5	592
Expenses	Photocopying	472	5	496
	Postages	984	5	1033
	Telephone	1336	5	1403
	Stationery	680	5	714
	Cars	1800	5	1890
	Typewriters	500	5	525
	Total	6336	5	6653

(iii) Premises expenses

(a) Rent

It may be that your premises are rented and a rent review is coming up: if not, then the rent will stay the same. If you have considered expanding, and you feel that within twelve months you might acquire additional accommodation, this should be quantified and included.

(b) Light, heat, rates, etc.

All these services are invariably the subject of lengthy discussion in the local and national press, and by the time you are actually considering your budget, you should know the proposed percentage increases.

(c) Finance

It may be that the requirements of the bank have not yet been identified, but let us assume that you have an overdraft of £2,500. If, however, you do not actually need to borrow money and even have more cash available than your immediate needs demand, then you can get investment advice from the bank.

(d) Insurance

With the help of the bank's expertise this figure should not only be easily identified, but possibly even reduced.

(e) Audit

Now that you are controlling your own expenditure, it is not unreasonable for you to expect other people to do the same with theirs - nor is it unreasonable to expect them to build in a similar growth to your own: 5 per cent would hardly keep up with inflation. You can see from Figure 3 that, on the above

Extract from Figure 3

		Last Year £	% Rise	Forecast £
Building	Rent	2750	0	2750
Expenses	Rates	688	5	722
	Electricity	176	5	185
	Gas	130	5	137
	Repairs	320	5	336
	Total.........................	4064		4130
Finance	Bank Interest	350	5	368
	Donations	15	5	16
	Insurance	275	5	289
	Auditors	750	5	788
	Advertising	1150	5	1208
	Depreciation	1395	–	1465
	Total.........................	3935	5	4134
Misc.	Course	85	5	89
	Entertainment	225	5	236
	Sundries	2750	5	2888
	Total.........................	3060	5	3213
	TOTAL EXPENSES	39895		42655
	PROFIT BEFORE TAX	6892		9279

basis, the expected increase in your expenses is to £42,655 or 7 per cent. It is worth bearing in mind, though, that when increasing wages, National Insurance contributions and PAYE will increase also.

4. MANUFACTURING OR RETAIL BUSINESS

The manufacturing and retail businesses are much the same as the service industry, but with two additions. These are stock and vehicles.

(i) Stock

Following the examination of last year's stock, it has been decided that better control could be exerted. The stock levels could also be reduced and purchases maintained at much the same level as last year. You will readily recognise from this that the stock levels are critical: if more stock is required, more cash will be tied up in the business. Remember: stock is not cash.

(ii) Vehicles

You can see from Figure 3 that, for the service industry, the anticipated cost of motor cars has been increased by 5 per cent. In a manufacturing business those figures might be a lot higher. In this example of a manufacturing business, the proprietor has instead decided to invest in a trailer which can be used more often. Additionally, it has been decided to use a car for towing purposes, thus reducing, at least for the immediate future, overall expenses.

5. FORECASTING TURNOVER

The exercise of forecasting and budgeting your expenses should make you appreciate that exactly the same predictions can be made for turnover. As has been suggested, once the shape of your business is known it should continue to perform in much the same way - but clearly if you take positive steps it will do even better.

(i) Service industries

In the service industry, repeat business may not always occur each year. It will be important for you to understand fully the levels and nature of your repeat business and to be realistic as to the likelihood of retaining it. Competition is ferocious in all businesses, but many professional and service sectors have been sheltered. It is assumed, for the purposes of this book, that a section of the core business (identified in Figure 4 as core group 1) is under attack in the longer term, but still has a reasonable growth over inflation for the next year.

Extract from Figure 4

Sales Mix	Last Year £	% Rise	Forecast £
Core Group 1	18715	10.5	20672
Core Group 2	16374	12.0	18339
Core Group 3	6082	10.0	6690
Core Group 4	4049	11.0	4494
Core Group 5	1567	11.0	1739
Total................	46787		51934

This attack on core business could take many forms depending on the general nature of the work undertaken. For solicitors, it could be conveyancing; pensions as opposed to life insurance in an insurance broking business; or the effects of the saturation of personal computers on the computer market. As a result, a conscious effort has to be made to diversify and, in the example, there is clearly scope for growth in groups 2 and 3, where figures of 12 per cent and 10 per cent respectively are forecast.

It has been necessary to consider each area of activity and make assumptions in respect of them. This exercise should not be carried out in isolation, but rather it should entail full discussion with everyone involved in the business. Do not forget that, at the end of the day, it is they who will have to achieve targets. A 10 per cent growth rate in our example may be considered a reasonable prospect and it certainly does no harm to be conservative about turnover, because it will subsequently identify the cash consequences (cash flow is discussed in Chapter Six). If you can live with the results on this basis, then any improvement in turnover should be considered a bonus.

(ii) Productive staff

Within the service industries, considerable reliance is placed on individuals of varying abilities. For the purposes of Figure 4 these are described as the owner and staff. It is assumed that the owner, along with a manager and two other members of staff, account for all the income. It is also assumed that a record has been kept of their individual contributions to the past year's turnover. If this has not been done, then it would be necessary to calculate their contribution from the invoices produced. This will give the kind of breakdown shown in Figure 4.

Extract from Figure 4

Productive Staff	Last Year £	Forecast £
Owner	23000	25530
Manager 1	17500	19425
Staff 1	4287	4759
Staff 2	2000	2220
Total	46787	51934

To calculate the forecast for the productive staff, multiply the previous year's figures by 51934/46787.

From the example, you can see that the owner produced £23,000. If there are to be no major changes in the productive staff, then the owner's contribution for the following year should be pro-rata to the forecast figure of £51,934. In that context, if the forecast of £51,934 is divided by last year's figure of £46,787, and then multiplied by the owner's last year figure of £23,000, he will have to achieve £25,530 for this year. A similar calculation can be made for all other staff.

(iii) Manufacturing and retail industries

Figure 15 shows the anticipated increase on the previous year's figures. Some attempt will be made to increase the contribution of the second core group, as it is felt that this is a reasonable area for diversification. However, to some extent sales are dictated by the anticipated stock levels and purchases, and manufacturing and retail industries must generate more turnover to accommodate their stock. If the shape of the business is known, however, cost control is more easily maintained, and such a growth is both realistic and achievable.

FIGURE 15: FORECAST ANALYSIS OF TURNOVER

	Last Year £	% Rise	Forecast £
Sales Mix			
Core Group 1	45000	10.0	49500
Core Group 2	39300	12.5	44219
Core Group 3	14597	10.0	16057
Core Group 4	10102	11.0	11213
Core Group 5	3288	11.0	3650
Total..........................	112287	11.0	124639

To simplify our calculations, the profits before tax in both sets of figures are approximately the same - namely £9,200 (see Figures 3 and 14).

6. COMPARISONS

Once you have established figures for the twelve months, it is then necessary to identify them on a monthly basis so that comparisons can be made. Your estimates, of course, will not be totally accurate, and so you will have to keep a close check on the figures. It would be pointless to have gone to all this trouble and then not use the information acquired. The next chapter deals with those comparisons and the appropriate steps which should be taken.

7. FUTURE PLANNING

If you accept that short and medium term planning can sometimes go wrong, then it seems logical that longer term planning is somewhat academic. If your twelve-month forecast is likely to be inaccurate, your five-year plan could be absolutely meaningless. However, you will by this stage have discovered that, simply by examining your annual figures, and giving them careful thought for the future, you have actually highlighted critical areas of your business. And as you have now established a shape, it will clearly be sensible to make an educated guess as to the future pattern. This could be on a year to year basis, but it is particularly interesting to plan for the longer term - say, five years ahead.

Even though the figures may well be wrong, therefore, the thought process involved will create an awareness and a direction for the future.

(i) Sales mix

Have a look at Figures 5 and 16. You can see that the first column of figures represents this current year's forecast and that the next set of figures represents the percentage increase that you consider reasonable for the following years.

Extract from Figure 16

SALES	Year 1 £	%	Year 2 £	%	Year 3 £	%	Year 4 £	%	Year 5 £
Core 1	49500	8	53460	7	57202	5	60062	3	61864
Core 2	44219	10	48641	8	52532	12	58836	13	66485
Core 3	16057	8	17342	8	18729	10	20602	11	22868
Core 4	11213	6	11886	6	12599	9	13733	10	15106
Core 5	3650	8	3942	8	4257	8	4598	8	4966
Total	124639		135271		145319		157831		171289

It is assumed that the business needs to be diversified, because as proprietor you believe that your principal business may be at risk. For this reason the core group 1 is run down over the period, while the core groups 2 and 3 are increased.

This exercise highlights one fairly fundamental principle. This is that if your valuable time is to be used in considering business plans, then it should be utilised to the maximum effect. Just look at the figures. You can see immediately that even an increase of only 2 per cent on either the first or second products will produce twice as much, say, as a 10 per cent increase on group 5. So it really does pay off for you to look at your principal business in order to make REAL improvements. You can also see that core groups 1 and 2 represent 75 per cent of your turnover - and you would probably find that they represent your principal customers too.

It is worth bearing in mind that you should not be too reliant on a small number of products, nor on just a few customers. When starting, you may have to rely on a handful of customers, but then it is often too difficult to cater for a large number. Do not forget that your entire production and energy are needed to look after those all important first customers. Obviously, you will do your best to expand your customer base, even if it means restricting sales to an existing customer, but it must be done carefully. You must achieve the right balance and that involves difficult decisions being made. But, if you want your business to grow, you will have to make them. Otherwise you might well find that you are totally vulnerable to your biggest customer, who can squeeze you both on price and delivery dates. If you fail to perform, this customer may find another supplier and then you may regret not having settled for a lower profit with a wider customer base. At least you would not have had all your eggs in one basket. When somebody said that there was no sentiment in business, he really knew what he was talking about.

The same also holds true for your suppliers. You should try to source your requirements from more than one supplier, though again this will not always be possible. It is not unheard of for a supplier actually to buy a business from a customer (namely yours), as a short cut to establishing his own service or manufacturing base. If you have had a good idea, imagine how you would feel selling out to your principal supplier at a knock-down price because he held you to ransom. So remember: commit yourself to a limited number of suppliers - possibly for as long as two or three years - but aim to broaden your customer base over your longer term plan, probably over five years.

(ii) Expenses
(a) Wages
Wages represent the largest source of expenditure, certainly in the service industries, and to a considerable extent in a manufacturing and retail business. In your own concern, no matter how much more modest, it will be extremely cost effective to give a careful and detailed consideration of your workforce and how they spend their time. Often, in a service industry, this is the only area where significant savings can be made, but however hard management tries these costs

always rise more quickly than was imagined. This is because additional staff not budgeted for are often required in a growing business, and an imbalance is created in respect of wage levels due to overtime and/or bonuses. For this reason the forecast rise in the wages cost is put at 9 per cent.

(b) Stock

The stock position is fundamental - and it is discussed in Chapter Five. For now, let us run over the basics. First, stock-taking should be done on a regular basis, although due to stock-levels this may only be possible quarterly. Taking stock regularly will identify obsolete or unsaleable stock - stock which, ultimately, it will be to your advantage to sell at a loss. Do not leave it taking up valuable floor space, and then more wasted time when it is to be checked again. After all, until it is sold, stock does not represent cash and a lower selling price is often better than nothing.

There are many reasonably priced computers on the market which can make stock control a lot easier, but get some advice before you rush out and buy one.

It is as well to have operated the systems described in this book on a manual basis, however, before embarking on the use of a computer. First you could have a look at the word-processing side which will introduce you to computers. Most new businesses need a typing facility, and many of the word-processing configurations are fairly straightforward, even if you feel you are a complete novice. In a new business, teenage sons and daughters may well have more than a passing ability, and you do not need to spend much initially - even a cheap machine will teach the rudiments of computing.

8. INFORMATION THE BANK WILL REQUIRE

(i) Copies of a forecast and budget for your business.

(ii) Assumptions
 (a) What are your major products or services?
 (b) Are your markets expanding or declining?
 (c) Have you any new products or services planned?
 (d) Who are your principal customers or clients?

(iii) Expenses
 (a) Reason for specific figures?
 (b) Will the forecast be compared with actuals on a monthly basis?

CHAPTER FIVE

ANALYSIS

1. INTRODUCTION

If you are going to the trouble of actually preparing forecasts of turnover and expenses, you must ensure that you use them. The whole principle behind preparing forecasts is to see how they compare with actual results. When you KNOW you have your forecast right, then your task is to ensure that it is achieved.

Frequently new businesses abandon their figure work simply because they fail to see the benefit of it once the necessary finance has been provided. Much of the trouble is caused because proprietors often have little or no input into the preparation of the figures. This is one of the most important jobs for a small business, yet it is all too often prepared by accountants or business agencies in isolation based on their assumptions rather than the owner's.

It is true that some small businesses have survived without such figures by merely relying on their bank balance from time to time. But it really is only some, and, of course, the bank balance reveals nothing about future commitments. In order that a business may be seen to be dynamic, it is essential for the owner to stand back and examine all aspects of the business on a regular basis. Quarterly is often enough. Provided you have kept the figures going and compared your actual results with your forecast, then you should never be taken by surprise. If the reality is that the business is not going to be successful, then it is probably just as well either to quit while you are ahead or cut your losses. Never throw good money after bad.

This chapter deals with the monthly considerations of your forecast, and of the financial consequences of your deliberations. The exercise is based either on your forecast resulting from last year's results, or from your best guess if you are starting up.

2. EXPENSES

There is no short cut in preparing a projection month by month. All expenses should now be known, and it should therefore be possible to prepare an analysis so that each payment falls in the appropriate month. Figures 6 and 17 set out how this can be achieved. Of course, some months have five weeks, and others four - a situation which changes from year to year.

(i) Wages

The split between wages and drawings is maintained. It is assumed that wages are paid weekly, and that the percentage increase is effective from the beginning of the new period.

(ii) Office expenses/postage

Unless the exercise has been done before, it may only be possible to analyse these on a straight-line basis. If you have a business which is very seasonal, or with heavy periods of mail-shots or correspondence, then you should, of course, identify the expenditure when you believe it will happen. All this has to be taken into account for other items under office expenses, and you will see that the telephone bill is paid quarterly.

(iii) Premises expenses

(a) Rent

This will fall in the months of payment, which are likely to be the usual quarter days - namely March 25, June 24, September 29 and December 25.

(b) Rates

Rates are paid on a straight-line basis for twelve months to

April. You should note though that rates payments may now be made by monthly instalments.

(c) *Lighting and heating*

The heaviest bills under this heading should occur during the winter months, although the British climate gives call to wonder where these periods actually begin and end. For the ease of our calculations, the costs are equal.

(d) *Repairs*

Unless you know the specific time when you are going to undertake such work, internal repairs and decorating tend to be done in the winter, and external repairs and decorating in the summer. If in doubt, then allocate a reasonable figure for this contingency.

(iv) Finance

(a) Bank charges and interest

These normally fall quarterly, on the usual quarter days, but will be entirely dependent on the type of financing you have arranged.

(b) Insurance

Insurance is usually paid annually. There is a provision in some cases to pay monthly, but at an increased cost.

(c) Audit

The auditors have agreed to be paid quarterly.

(d) Advertising

Expenditure on advertising will clearly fluctuate with your market and is unlikely to be the same each month, particularly if your trade is seasonal, but for simplicity's sake, it is calculated here on a straight line.

(e) Depreciation

This has been included in the expenses to highlight the real cost of running the business, but as it does not represent an actual cash payment it has been included in the April figure, otherwise it would confuse your cash flow calculation.

(v) Sundries
Again, for simplicity's sake, these may have to be inserted on a straight-line basis.

(vi) Total
The total of each column identifies the expenditure each month.

3. PURCHASES
Manufacturing and retail businesses rely on stock. Indeed, if it was not for stock, there would not be a business at all. But it is still an expense and is included in the expenses. The actual stock figures are highlighted in the projections, but have not been added into the total. Stock figures will be included in the cash flow.

4. TURNOVER
Before an analysis can be made of the results, a similar exercise will have to be carried out for your turnover. Figures 7 and 18 show a proposed breakdown but, without actually knowing the type of business involved, it is impossible to do anything more than merely establish the principle.

(i) Sales mix
The target must be achieved one way or another. It is as simple as that. The end justifies the means and, in a retail business, the year end leading up to the January sales may - along with the mid-summer sales - be the means for success and consequently the heaviest periods. Conversely, in an engineering business these may be the quietest times. In professional and service industries any such seasonal flux may well be less apparent.

(ii) Total
Whatever your assessment might be, each column is totalled

to give the anticipated sales for each month.

5. COST OF SALES

In a service industry, the gross profit figure can be achieved each month by simply deducting the expenses for the appropriate month from the actual sales.

In a manufacturing or retail business this is not quite so easy to deduce because of stock. The only way of reaching an appropriate profit figure is by taking stock regularly. The use of a computer for regular stock control is essential - indeed without it, the exercise just may not be realistic at all. It can, however, be done manually if you are careful. Whatever way you do it, you must keep a very close control on stock, and experience will dictate the appropriate levels.

Given that you have prepared a forecast which, on present figures, assumes that your gross profits will represent 42 per cent of sales, then you can identify the anticipated gross profit each month. In Figure 19 you will see that the sales in May were £7,280 and that 42 per cent of that is £3,057. This is the figure which is used in the monthly and quarterly profit calculations.

6. ANALYSING RESULTS

Now that you have prepared a projection of turnover and expenses for each month, it is possible to compare your actual results with your forecast. Figures 8 and 19, for example, show the results for the months to June.

(i) Sales

This shows the target for the month, which is taken directly from Figures 7 and 18 under the June heading.

(ii) Actual

This represents the actual results for the period which are almost on target. Not very surprising really, as this is only the second month of the period. Your sales were probably known for May when you prepared the forecast, and you would have a fairly good idea of the likely results for June. This good and accurate beginning could well deteriorate as the year progresses.

FIGURE 19: ANALYSING PERFORMANCE

	A Annual Budget £	B Actual May £	C Budget June £	D Actual June £	E Variance June (D-C) £	F Year To Date (B+D) £
SALES						
Core Group 1	49500	2750	3250	3450	200	6200
Core Group 2	44219	2630	3000	3200	200	5830
Core Group 3	16057	975	1325	1125	−200	2100
Core Group 4	11213	750	657	875	218	1625
Core Group 5	3650	175	215	127	−88	302
Total Sales.........	124639	7280	8447	8777	330	16057
Purchases.........	76590	4750	5000	4750	−250	9500
Gross Profit @ 42% of Sales	51934	3057	3547	3686	139	6743
EXPENSES						
Wages	24525	2320	1856	1856	0	4176
Office	6653	1296	304	452	148	1748
Building	4130	60	748	755	7	815
Finance	4194	322	217	196	−21	518
Misc.	3213	396	222	235	13	631
Total.............	42715	4394	3347	3494	147	7888
PROFIT BEFORE TAX	9219	−1337	200	192	−8	−1145

(iii) Difference (+ or -)

This highlights the accuracy of your forecast. In the present results there is nothing too dramatic. If, however, the sales were lower than expected, then you should make inquiries to find out why. For example, a member of staff may have been absent through illness; a machine may have broken down; or there may have been adverse weather conditions. The cause must be found and the appropriate action taken.

(iv) Expenses

These need to be carefully compared and similar considerations applied to the results.

(v) Year to date

This is a cumulative total of the May and actual June figures. In the example, it is assumed that the projected results in Figures 6, 7, 17 and 18 for May are the actual results. These figures become more useful in subsequent years for annual comparisons.

(vi) Purchases (in Figure 19)

As explained earlier, these also need comparing with your forecast.

(vii) Gross profit

So that a gross profit figure can be struck, it is assumed that the gross profit percentage mentioned earlier still applies - that figure is 42 per cent. We then deduct the annual expenses, giving a profit before tax of £192 for the period. We have talked already about stock control and stock-taking, but it is worth remembering that a stock-taking at least half way through the year is essential. More frequently would be a considerable advantage.

7. QUARTERLY PROFIT AND LOSS ACCOUNT

The monthly results (discussed above) will not reveal likely trends as readily and as obviously as quarterly results. Figures 9 and 20 show the position at the end of the first three months, and much the same comments apply as have already been made with regard to the month end figure.

When considering the figures, it is important to decide whether the three months under consideration are truly representative. It may be that there are considerable movements in your sales figure, in which case a good quarter may be followed by a quieter period or vice versa. Similarly, some expenses which relate to the whole year may not yet

Extract from Figure 9

		Budget £	Actual £	Variance £
Income	Core Group 1	4100	4250	150
	Core Group 2	3525	3750	225
	Core Group 3	1060	1200	140
	Core Group 4	850	765	−85
	Core Group 5	415	387	−28
	Total	9950	10352	402

have been included. A relative portion of these, of course, should be taken into account to obtain an accurate figure. For example, in the present figures there is no allowance made for depreciation. This amount will actually be taken into account in April at the year end, but it would be far more accurate to apportion this expense equally across the entire trading period.

8. WHAT IF?

The whole purpose of the comparisons is not only to see what *is* happening, but also what might happen. If you have familiarised yourself with a word-processor, you might now take the opportunity of learning to work what is called a spread sheet. As the squares can hold numbers or letters it is possible to set up a model of your forecast in which the figures change as you change the assumptions.

Looking at Figure 6, if all the sheet is interrelated, a change anywhere on the screen will alter all the subsequent figures. This can save a great deal of time and will allow you to insert different assumptions in order to see what will happen. For example: "What if I increase my wage bill by 15 per cent instead of 9 per cent?" Immediately the computer will recalculate the full year with the new figures substituted. Most good computers have a spread sheet application, but you will probably have to allow some time to familiarise yourself with the appropriate programme.

9. SALES MIX

On the present forecast (see Figures 9 and 20) the businesses are essentially on course. But it may be that the sales have not been achieved in one of the core groups.

It will be recalled that you are able to record new work as it actually comes into the business (see Figures 2 and 13) which will provide a considerable lead time by alerting you to improvements or depressions in the market. You can then calculate *what* is likely to happen *if* matters continue to follow the same trends. As a result you will be able to react to market place conditions quickly. If you know that a specific area of your sales is falling, and you have little prospect of changing the position in the short to medium term, then you are left with two choices:

(i) To re-allocate executive or machine time to alternative activity, or

(ii) To attempt to reduce your costs - either within this department or within the firm generally.

Having made different assumptions about the future, you are able to feed the figures into your model in order to ascertain the consequences. If the answer is unacceptable, you will either have to change your plan or cut your losses as best you can.

It may be that the crisis is short term (possibly a disruption in the supply of your raw materials, or the weather) and the bank could well help you. In the light of these events you may have to re-calculate your cash flow and the next chapter deals with the preparation of a cash flow forecast. If, for example, you anticipate that your sales will recover later in the year, the bank might well finance you in the short term. In any event, the bank will be much happier to be approached before the problem arises, or at least as soon as it is discovered, and may have some useful and helpful suggestions to make.

10. EXPENSES

On the forecast set out in Figures 9 and 20 there are no major problems. It has been suggested earlier that there could be difficulties in relation to sales, but if this is the case it will be essential to look at expenses to see if any savings can be made. In a service industry there is no doubt that very little can be done in the short term. This is principally because you will be committed to a given level of employees and so it is wise to choose your employees with extreme care.

11. FIVE-YEAR PLAN

As your figures become available you may well find that you need to reconsider some of your earlier thoughts which gave rise to your five-year plan.

12. PROFITABILITY

Do not forget WHY you are running your own business: to make a profit. If you do not make enough profit, you have wasted your time and energy - you might just as well be working for somebody else. It may be that some of the benefits are not cash ones, but all the same benefits which give you genuine satisfaction. You may consider it worth, say, £2,000 or even more just to be your own boss. You may also feel that ultimately you may be able to sell the business you have built up. All this could be true, but do not take this line of reasoning too far. Be realistic, and remember that if you work for somebody else:

> (i) You would not need to invest your hard-earned money in your business at all. Instead, you could put it safely on deposit and collect interest.

> (ii) You would undoubtedly be paid a wage in line with the market place.

> (iii) You might even expect your employer to make a substantial contribution to a pension.

This is what you are aiming for. This is why you are in business! When you have only been in it for a short time, it is unlikely that your business will fulfil all your ambitions immediately. But unless one of your goals - profitability - is at least in sight, you could be in serious trouble.

13. ADVANTAGES OF FIGURES

Another advantage of having the figures in the form suggested in this book is that you can easily and quickly calculate the profitability of individual departments. This can often be a very revealing exercise, as you can see from Figures 5 and 16 which contain the breakdown of the anticipated sales mix and expenses. It is possible to work out the actual costs of producing the results in each of those areas, but you will have to make the following allocations:

(i) The labour content - both direct and salary.
(ii) The overhead content.
(iii) The stock at cost (in the case of a manufacturing or retail business).

Where a cost cannot be specifically allocated (such as a general overhead), then this should be expressed on a pro-rata basis.

Margins by Departments

		£	
Core Group 1.	Forecast for year to 1988	20672	
	£		
Actual wages	8660		
Actual Expenses	6978		
Overhead Wages	1150	16788	
		3884	(margin 19%)

For margins by departments (see Figure 5), core group 1 represents 40 per cent of the total forecast turnover (£20,672 divided by £51,934). The actual wages reflect what was paid to the labour force for producing this turnover. The actual expenses are 40 per cent of the total overhead expenses of the office, premises, finance and sundries (ie. 40 per cent of £17,445 is £6,978). The overhead wage is 40 per cent of those wages which cannot be identified to any particular department. These include telephonists, cashiers and general staff, who assist all departments. The resulting expense of £16,788 leaves a contribution to profit of £3,884. This is 19 per cent of the turnover for the department (ie. £3,884 divided by £20,672). If you want to improve this to 25 per cent (£5,168) of the current turnover figure, you will either have to reduce costs by £1,284 or increase the turnover by the same amount.

From the above you will see that for every £1 of turnover in this core group, 19p is actual profit. In the text it is suggested that the sales in core group 1 have peaked and are beginning to fall. If they fell to £16,788 - which is the level of expenses for the entire department - then you would be making no profit at all. You would merely be breaking even. But that may not necessarily matter because the department is making a contribution to the overhead expenses (£6,978 + £1,150). But if the sales fell still further, you could only retain your margin by reducing the work force. The bottom line is that it could be inevitable that you would reach a point where you really are losing money. Then you would clearly be well advised to close down the department.

Despite pressure in the market place to do so, you need not necessarily reduce your price. Instead, if you reduce your cost and maintain your price, you could actually make the same profit, even in a falling market. More importantly, you might well have reorganised your work force so that they are profitably employed in some other department. This sort of calculation can often highlight anomalies.

Time is at a premium and it simply is not possible to investigate all the permutations and calculate all the possible variations, but there is no doubt that if you deal with the principal ones your business can improve dramatically. Again, a spread sheet can be set up to work out the variations for you, so that you can feed in the appropriate figures as they occur.

14. CONCLUSION

The figures to date only reveal your best estimates when compared with your actual results. But they do not necessarily indicate the level of cash in the business. It is, however, necessary to have prepared these figures in order to enable you to prepare a cash forecast - which is discussed in the next chapter.

15. QUESTIONS TO ASK YOURSELF IN PREPARING FORECASTS

(i) Are the general objectives of the business still the same? If not, where do they differ? And what do I propose to do about it?

(ii) Have I sufficient expertise within my organisation to cover the following?

> General management.
> Sales.
> Production.
> Finance.

(iii) Can I contain or reduce my costs without affecting quality or volume?

CHAPTER SIX

CASH FLOW

1. INTRODUCTION

In spite of all the figures and the previous forecasts, the cash generated by the business does not always bear any relationship either to sales or expenses. Cash is the life blood of any business, and many profitable and sound concerns have fallen on hard times because they failed to understand its importance.

It is not possible to assess your cash situation until you have completed all the figures referred to in the earlier chapters. And, of course, any possible help you might hope for from the bank will be entirely dependent on those figures. But, assuming you have produced the figures, then you can produce a cash flow forecast.

There is nothing mystical in preparing a cash flow forecast. It is a logical extension of the forecasting principles and, as before, the mere exercise of actually preparing such a statement can be very revealing.

2. THE CALCULATION

You are referred to Figures 10 and 21. Basically, the form starts with details of everything coming in - all the cash receipts of any nature identified under each appropriate month. Beneath those are details of everything going out - all items of cash expenditure.

It has been decided that the bank will be asked to inject an additional £4,250 for capital expenditure. In spite of a temptation to finance this out of your current cash position, you should understand that it is not sound business procedure to fund longer term capital expenditure out of current income. This is not just because it distorts the true profit, but because such an unnecessary tying-up of funds

FIGURE 10: CASH FLOW

	May £	June £	Jul £	Aug £	Sep £	Oct £	Nov £	Dec £	Jan £	Feb £	Mar £	Apr £
INCOME												
Debtors/Cash Sale	2478	2696	3184	2830	2703	3238	4022	2824	4981	4632	5299	4738
VAT received	438	475	562	503	477	572	717	496	878	823	941	844
Capital Introduced	0	0	0	0	0	0	0	0	0	500	0	0
Other Cash	440	472	560	525	475	575	755	485	875	855	975	890
Bank Loan	4250	0	0	0	0	0	0	0	0	0	0	0
Total .... (A)	7606	3643	4306	3858	3655	4385	5494	3805	6734	6810	7215	6472
PAYMENTS												
Expenses	3870	2928	2680	2524	3095	2993	2345	4066	3061	2389	3092	2697
Drawings	375	375	375	375	375	375	375	375	375	375	375	375
Loan Repayment	0	120	120	120	120	120	120	120	120	120	120	120
VAT	0	1344	0	0	1557	0	0	1800	0	0	2663	0
Tax	0	0	506	0	0	0	0	0	506	0	0	0
Capital items	4250	0	0	0	0	0	0	0	0	0	0	0
Total .... (B)	8495	4767	3681	3019	5147	3488	2840	6361	4062	2884	6250	3192
CASH FLOW (A−B)	−889	−1124	625	839	−1492	897	2654	−2556	2672	3926	965	3280
BANK BALANCE b/f	−2500	−3389	−4513	−3888	−3049	−4541	−3644	−990	−3546	−874	3052	4017
BANK BALANCE c/f	−3389	−4513	−3888	−3049	−4541	−3644	−990	−3546	−874	3052	4017	7297

could leave the business exposed to a shortage of cash when it is most needed.

How much you can actually borrow will depend on a variety of matters but, if the proposition is sound - and particularly if it can be backed with security, such as your home - then the bank may advance you two to three pounds for every pound you can put up. A loan for its own sake is not necessarily a good idea, however. If you can manage with less borrowing, but without leaving yourself short of cash, you should try to do so. Remember that all borrowings have to be repaid eventually - and also remember that it does cost money to borrow money. If you borrow more than your business can reasonably sustain, the result could be disastrous. And, of course, borrowing is, all too often, a means of postponing the inevitable. Firms which find themselves severely under-financed should concentrate on improving their trading position, not borrowing money to help them in the short term.

Capital funding is discussed in Chapter Seven, and Figures 10 and 21 deal predominantly with the anticipated income position for the present year. The capital injection is anticipated to be repaid over three years at £120 per month. If you are aware that capital is to be introduced, it may be easier to work out how much you need - and how best the business can finance it - after you have worked out an initial cash flow. If the figures are on your spread sheet then it is a great deal easier.

(i) Debtors and cash sales

These are calculated from the projection of turnover contained in Figures 7 and 18. The projections in those figures are, of course, not cash projections, but merely invoiced sales or fees.

Not all invoiced sales will be paid at once and, although when you complete your first sales you will receive some cash immediately, many of your customers or clients will take credit. Some may settle their debt within sixty days while others will take longer and you will receive that cash in the following month. But, of course, some may not pay you at all!

Your balance sheet (see Figures 11 and 22) will show how much money was owed to you by your customers (debtors) at the year end. You should calculate the length of time debtors take to pay you in the following way:

(a) Calculate the average daily sales by dividing the turnover for the last year by 365.
(b) Divide the resulting figure into your debtors on the balance sheet, and this will show you how many days of sales they represent.

You may well be surprised how long these are, although it should be possible to work on two months. However, if some of your debtors are exceeding this time, you may be able to improve your cash position merely by actively pressing customers to pay you more quickly. In fact, you should always try to do this anyway. It requires no greater turnover, nor expense, and is discussed in more depth later in this chapter. Remember: you must be aware of how quickly you are paid in relation to your invoices. Just as cash is the life blood of your business, bad circulation has been known to be a cause of death.

If your debtors represent two months' sales, this is 16 per cent of your turnover. For the purposes of the cash flow chart, the projected sales in Figures 7 and 18 have been reduced by 16 per cent.

(ii) VAT

The level at which you need to register for VAT varies from Budget to Budget. The figures used in this book(Figures 10 and 21) assume that you are registered for VAT and that you will also be receiving some VAT, as some invoices are paid each month, both from the original sales and cash. The cash will be received as the bill is paid so that in May, 15 per cent of £2,478 and 15 per cent of £440 (totalling £437.90 or £438 for ease of simplicity) will be received additionally for VAT. The forecast of fees is exclusive of VAT. Small businesses can currently elect to pay VAT on a cash received rather than a bills delivered basis, and they can also elect to complete one return each year, but actually pay only an average VAT monthly. Whether you should make this election needs careful consideration as it assumes that your cash receipts will be even, which of course is not the case. It also assumes that you will actually receive more VAT than you pay which is not always so. Seek advice from your accountant or the bank.

(iii) Other cash

If your customers are taking time to pay, you will also receive in each month part of the sales from the previous two months. It is likely that 2/3rds of the outstanding money will be paid at the end of the subsequent month, and the remaining 1/3rd the month after. Thus, the cash receipts in July represent May's final 1/3rd payments and June's first 2/3rds payments. If you anticipate capital receipts - either in the form of cash injected by you or as a loan from the bank - the amount so introduced should appear here.

(iv) Total

If you received interest from the bank, arising on deposits, commission or other income, it should appear in the appropriate months prior to totalling each, otherwise the totals will appear as in Figures 10 and 21.

(v) Expenses

These are itemised in Figures 6 and 17 but represent in this chart the total at the end of each month. Interest and capital repaid to the bank appear here, as do purchases.

In the manufacturing and retail industries, account will have to be taken of the purchase of stock. It was for this reason that Figure 17 carried a detail of the purchases, as these are, of course, a major expense and are carried to Figure 21.

(vi) Drawings

As we discussed in Chapter Four, all businesses should generate sufficient money to pay a reasonable wage to their owners. When you start up in business, you will find, particularly over the first two years, that your drawings will have been severely restricted. That position should not, however, continue for any length of time or difficulties may occur in the longer term.

It might be as well to assess the cash flow position before taking drawings, but in the figures, a provision of £375 a month has been made for drawings. You will note that £5,450 was forecasted for drawings - see Figures 3 and 14. This amount appears in the forecast under wages so that a correct profit can be struck and carried to the forecast of actual expenses - see Figures 6 and 17. For the purposes of the cash flow calculation the drawings figure has been taken off the wages figure in Figures 10 and 21. Instead a cash drawing of £375 has been included and tax taken out in addition of £1,012. If, when the calculations are finished, you discover that the overdraft is too high, these drawings could be reduced in the short term or waived altogether.

(vii) **VAT payments**

You will know and budget for all dates by which VAT must be paid: they usually occur in three-month cycles. Remember though that this includes the VAT on all your invoices, whether they are paid or not, less any VAT paid out by you in running your business.

(viii) **Income tax**

We will be discussing tax in more detail in Chapter Eight, but a limited company pays nine months after its year end. The amount to be paid is assessed on the firm's preceding year's taxable profit. There are different rules for dividend payments, when corporation tax is payable in advance - usually within 14 days of the end of a "return period" (a "return period" is usually a calendar quarter). It is extremely unlikely that a dividend payment would be made in the first few years of a new company's trading life unless there were outside shareholders who require such a payment. In a partnership or sole trader concern, tax is payable on January 1 and July 1 of each year. As a result the proprietor can only be assessed to tax after his profits are known - usually one year in arrear. If staff are employed, pay as you earn (PAYE) tax is due as the wages are paid, and is accounted for by the proprietor to the Inland Revenue in accordance with the PAYE tables specifically provided for that purpose. As the Government is always examining the rates payable and how income tax and corporation tax are assessed, changes are inevitable.

(ix) Total

Unless there are other items of expenditure, each month is totalled showing the total cash payments.

(x) Surplus (+) and deficit (-)

The resultant figure is deducted from the total receipts giving either a surplus or deficit. Obviously, if payments exceed income, you will end up with a deficit. If income is more than payments, then you have a surplus.

(xi) Bank balance (+) or (-)

Assume, for the purpose of Figures 10 and 21, that the business currently has a trading overdraft of £2,500.

(xii) Cash flow

As May shows a deficit in both sets of accounts, the deficit is added to the preceding bank balance of £2,500, thus revealing a total deficit of £3,389 in Figure 10 and a deficit of £3,330 in Figure 21.

In order to calculate the resulting cash balances for the year, you need only carry the deficit (or surplus) forward, and add it to, or subtract it from, the following month. From this it will be noted that the service industry's highest indebtedness is in September - amounting to £4,541 which changes by the end of the year to £7,297. (It should be remembered that depreciation of £1,465 is deducted from the forecast as an expense, but as this is not actually cash, it should be ignored in the cash flow forecast). The manufacturing and retail industry's highest indebtedness is in June - amounting to £5,634. At the end of the year its cash position is very much better, and actually shows a credit of £2,930.

3. IMPLICATIONS

You should now consider the implications of the forecast. The main object of being in business is to generate sufficient cash, not merely to help to finance growth but to improve the actual value of the business for the owners. A full analysis is therefore clearly important in order to ascertain what scope there could be for improvement.

(i) Sales

Any improvement in sales, no matter how slight, could increase income significantly, and it may be possible for you to reconsider your pricing structures. Certainly, you could always test the market for a short time.

(ii) Debtors

A little early care can save a lot of problems later and you would be well advised to exercise a formal control of your customers, preferably before you actually take them on. Status inquiries on your behalf may be made by the bank - either before entering into an agreement or simply extending credit limits. Any reluctance on your part in requesting money owed to you is not justified. Clearly, if a debt is several months old, you would be irresponsible to allow the customer any more credit, although it is unlikely that he or she will come back to you while the debt is outstanding. Remember:

(a) If you can obtain any portion of the amount outstanding, then do so.

(b) Send out a reminder for each outstanding invoice.

(c) After a reasonable time, which you yourself must decide, send out a second reminder for all unpaid bills - but this time make it out entirely in red ink. Quite frequently customers react to red reminders.

(d) Do not be afraid to make telephone calls or even personal visits during this period of reminders. You are entitled to make any reasonable attempt to ascertain why you are not being paid. You may be able to help alleviate any worries over financial difficulties simply by calling round and suggesting a schedule of part repayments until the position improves.

(e) If none of these methods produces any reasonably tangible results, then you need to recognise that your money is very much at risk and you should call in professional help. Assuming the customer has paid you by cheque in the past, it would be worthwhile asking the bank to make a status inquiry of your customer's bank to see if he has sufficient funds for payment. If this proves negative, then you should ensure that your customer can raise the money before you go any further. If you do decide to proceed, you might consider instructing a professional collection agency. Or you may feel that a letter from your solicitor may extract payment.

Whatever course of action you decide to try, you should always remember that in order to get your money you might have to take the debtor to court. If your customer goes bankrupt or goes into liquidation, you ought to be able to recover the VAT. Of course, by this time the debt could well have been outstanding for more than 18 months.

(iii) Creditors

Creditors are the people to whom you owe money. When paying bills always remember how you would wish your debtors to behave. Take advantage of any discounts which may be offered, of course, but do not take extended credit unless there is no alternative. If you do, you will be financing your business out of your creditors and, unless you are keeping a very tight control on your finances, you will undoubtedly run the risk of having to pay out excessive amounts when you can least afford it. In difficult times, however, your supplier - whom you will probably be paying every six weeks - will be more likely to take care of you if you are a good payer. But remember: why should he, like you, take any risks?

(iv) Discounts

You should examine carefully all discounts offered by your

suppliers. Wherever possible, always use the discount which is likely to give you the largest saving.

(v) Stock control
The amount of money tied up in stock can be considerable. In a manufacturing industry this will represent:

(a) Raw material held to accommodate production.

(b) Raw material being worked and absorbed in the work in progress.

(c) Finished stock awaiting either delivery or customers. As explained earlier, a tight control should be taken of stock to make sure that it is neither slow-moving nor obsolete.

It is hoped that, by understanding fully the way in which your business functions, you can ensure that all work is progressed by the right people, in the right place AND at the right time.

4. THE BALANCE SHEET
When running your business on a day to day basis, you will be preoccupied in making sure that sufficient cash is being generated to keep it going. At some stage - if not all the time! - you will want to know whether you are trading profitably, and this is where the balance sheet comes in.

The balance sheet sets out the position of your business on a given day and it cannot therefore be looked at in isolation. Have a look at Figures 11 and 22, which are the balance sheets for both types of business as at April 30.

We have assumed that in both cases there is a balance to carry forward from the previous year, and that the owner of each business has been able, during the current year, to put £500 into the business. Added to that amount is the profit for the year (taken from the forecast in Figure 3) of £9,279. For the sake of completeness, although it is irrelevant where there is only one owner, interest of 12 per cent on the original £500 has been added, so that the balance of the profit available is £9,219. If the business gets bigger and other partners join -

and the contribution to the capital is unequal - then it may be necessary to add interest first.

The owner has been drawing £375 per month which amounts to £4,500 in the year. As these are fairly new businesses it has not been possible for the owner to draw out any more money and there will, of course, be the tax liability which will overlap this year and last. All that remains in the business is the balance on the capital account - namely £17,129 in Figure 11 and £14,623 in Figure 22. It is now necessary for you to balance that figure with the other assets in the business.

(i) Fixed assets

Fixed assets represent the items acquired by the owner to enable him or her to run the business.

(a) Leasehold interest

It is not very often that a lease has any significant value at the beginning of the term although it is possible for the premises to have been acquired under circumstances in which the owner would expect an "in going" to be paid by somebody else. The most usual situation, however, is where the property was derelict, and both money and time have been expended in order to make them usable. For our example, it is assumed that the premises for the service business are worth £2,750, and in the manufacturing business, slightly less (the standard of office accommodation in a service industry business will usually be superior).

You will recall that depreciation must be taken into account. The lease is only for five years and at the end of that period you may feel that it will be of no value to this business as it will revert to the landlord. But this is not altogether true. In most cases, the tenant will be protected under the Landlord and Tenant Act 1954 Part II, unless the landlord advised the tenant (and the County Court) that security would not be given. The rules are quite complicated and you should seek legal advice, but then that is true of every case before you enter into a lease. As the lease time remaining is so short, depreciation at the rate of 20 per cent has been applied and, in fact, depreciation at that rate has been deducted from all fixed assets.

(b) Machinery and office equipment

This represents all items of furniture purchased for the business, less depreciation. Of course, you do not always need to buy your furniture - it is possible to lease all these items. While this would save on the initial cash outlay, however, the rental costs would increase your monthly outgoings. And if the business runs into difficulties, the rented items may well be repossessed by the owners. In view of the fairly small amount spent it is probably sensible to buy these items, but you may be well advised to check out the market before making any firm commitments. A manufacturing business will also need plant in the form of machinery.

(c) Motor cars/vehicles

Some sort of transportation will be an essential, although its value and size will depend not only on your priorities, but also on what you think your customers or clients might expect. In the early, formative years of your business, reliability is probably the most important consideration. For example, if you are in a manufacturing business - and provided the product is not too large - it might be an idea to buy an estate car and a trailer. At least in that way you will have something you can use when you are not working; the same cannot, of course, be said of a van or truck. In our example, it has been assumed that very modest vehicles have been acquired.

(ii) Current assets

All the items discussed so far are of a tangible nature, and are clearly essential for the operation of the business. But there are other assets to consider, too.

(a) Stock/work in progress

In a manufacturing or retail business there will be stock, and the stock on hand at any one time will represent three stages of your business operation: raw materials, work in progress and finished goods. In our example, these amount to £21,385, which is taken from the forecast in Figure 14. At the year end (and regularly throughout the year!) stock will be physically valued. If you add the closing stock to the opening stock and divide by two you will get the average stock for the year: thus £21,385 + £17,500 = £38,885 divided by 2 = £19,442.

If you then divide the result into the figure for the purchases, you will discover that this business turns over its stock every three months (ie. £76,590 divided by £19,442 = 4). Of course, whether this is good enough depends on the trade you are in.

In a service industry business you will probably be asked to value your work in progress and this will entail valuing all the jobs within the business at the year end. As you will be entitled to no profit at that stage - because none of the jobs in progress is actually finished - the jobs should be valued with a proportion of the overheads and the wages included as appropriate.

(b) Debtors

As explained earlier, the business will be owed money by its customers and clients. The turnover for the service business is forecast at £51,934 (Figure 3). This means that sales at the rate of £998 per week are expected, so the debtors figure of £5,238 represents five weeks credit (£5,238 divided by £998 = 5.25), which is not too bad for a new business. You can see that, if this can be reduced to four weeks, then £998 will be introduced into the business at no extra cost or effort. Clearly, if you can work entirely on cash, you will do very well.

(c) Balance at bank

The service industry is running in credit with a balance of £7,297.

The forecast cash flow for the manufacturing and retail business is, however, rather worse. The cash anticipated at the bank for them is £2,930, but it should be remembered that VAT for two months is outstanding and must be paid at the end of next month, and also that stock has not yet been paid for.

In the previous month the balance at the bank was £2,955 overdrawn: in fact it is conceivable that this balance may not actually be achieved at the year end. This is a clear demonstration of why a balance sheet has to be considered with some care.

(iii) Current liabilities

In order for the figures to balance, you must deduct any amount owed by the business, but not yet paid at the end of the year. All these figures will differ depending on what date is taken.

(a) Creditors

In the service business, the figure is £2,365 with the anticipated expenses for the year at £42,655.

(b) Income tax

Tax is payable on the preceding year's figures, but in the case of a new business tax will be payable on an estimated figure. In any event, tax will be payable in January and July of each year. In our example, we assume that tax is payable and that this will be the balance of the tax for the preceding year in the case of the sole trader or partnership, namely £506.

(c) Bank loan

You will remember that the bank lent the business £4,250 to be repaid at £120 per month, with the first payment being due the first month after the loan was made. Assuming, for ease of calculation, that this is capital only, then £1,320 will have been paid leaving £2,930 outstanding. It will also be recalled that the interest element has been paid in the expenses (see Figures 3 and 14).

5. INFORMATION THE BANK WILL REQUIRE

(i) Have you prepared a cash flow?
(ii) What assumptions have you made with regard to debtors, creditors and stock?

CHAPTER SEVEN

SOURCES OF FINANCE

1. LOANS FROM THE BANK

As you have now completed a cash flow forecast you will have a reasonable idea of your cash requirements. Figures 10 and 21 set out the likely cash requirements for both businesses and you need to decide on the particular form of finance you require.

(i) Overdraft

A distinction should be made between actual capital and revenue requirements. In the case of acquiring an asset which is likely to be used in the business over a longer term, then it would be unreasonable for this purchase to be financed out of only one year's income. It is particularly important that the business attempts to keep within its cash limits, and in doing so it is not always sensible to spend all your available cash which could, of course, be needed to run your business.

If we assume for the moment that both of the businesses in our example have no major capital expenditure, then the extent of the overdraft would be the maximum liability revealed in the cash forecast. Whether the bank would require security for such an overdraft would depend on both the trading record to date and the value of the business as a whole. But if your business has sufficient assets to cover your loan, then the bank may not require further security.

You should appreciate, however, that capital assets have a low liquidity - in other words, they cannot easily or quickly be transformed into hard cash - and the bank may well seek to secure assets which are more liquid. Remember too that an overdraft is repayable on demand although, as long as the bank remains confident and is constantly informed of your situation and advised of your requirements, there is no reason why it should not exist for a long time. Having prepared forecasts, the bank will expect you to keep them informed, at least on a quarterly basis, thus enabling an ongoing comparison to be made of your forecast with your actual results, which can be important both for the bank and yourself.

(ii) Short term loan

Where capital expenditure can adequately be repaid in two or three years, the bank will be disposed to lend an agreed sum, for repayment over a specified period. Interest will be payable at an agreed rate over the bank's current base rate. The rate of interest is a matter for negotiation and if security can be given, such as a house or stocks and shares, the rate may be reduced because the risk to the bank is less. Clearly, it will be necessary in your application to the bank to identify the purpose of the loan and the basis of repayment.

(iii) Medium term loan

Much the same considerations apply to this as to the short term loan, though this may run for up to five years. In some circumstances the bank may agree a fixed rate of interest of a lower percentage, but payable on the full loan for its entire duration. It may also agree a "holiday" period - when no capital repayments are necessary.

(iv) Long term loan

Long term loans will usually only be given in those circumstances where large capital funding is required. Repayment can be over terms as long as 20 years, but security will be necessary and the bank will need to be satisfied that the repayment schedule can be maintained.

(v) Debentures

In the case of limited companies, the bank may be prepared to take a floating charge over all the company's assets as security. Called a debenture, the charge enables the bank to have first claim on the value of the whole business should the company fail to comply with the agreed terms. Meanwhile, the company is free to operate within the terms of the arrangement.

There will be a fixed charge on all the company's properties, and a floating charge on all its intangible assets. If, for example, the money owed to the company is £25,000 (debtors), or stock is £40,000, then the bank may well allow a percentage of those figures in arriving at the facility. The bank will undoubtedly want management figures on a regular basis, so that it can monitor the position from time to time.

(vi) Additional finance

The bank will have experience in the factoring of debts and leasing. There are some occasions when debt factoring is more attractive than normal banking arrangements. This involves the lender in the purchase of a proportion of your debts for immediate cash. The lender then collects them in, and pays you the balance less a handling charge.

(vii) Leasing

It is often sensible to acquire capital assets by way of lease, particularly where the technology is moving quickly. Items such as photocopying machines, electronic typewriters and computers, as well as high-tech production machinery, are worthy of such consideration. The bank has considerable experience in this area and is always willing to help.

2. GOVERNMENT ASSISTANCE

A considerable amount of Government assistance is available, and the bank is well able to advise on the various schemes currently active. It is not worthwhile identifying these schemes in any detail here because they change from time to time, but as a general rule note that preference is given to manufacturing businesses in development areas.

3. LOAN GUARANTEE SCHEME

The purpose of the Loan Guarantee Scheme is to enable the bank to support your application when personal security is not available. The loans may be from two to seven years with up to a two-year capital repayment holiday. The maximum amount that may be borrowed under the scheme varies, and the interest rates are agreed with the bank. The Government also makes a charge by way of additional interest for the guarantee and this can make the borrowing very expensive - particularly at a time when funds are scarce - which may be a high price to pay to cover the risk.

4. GRANTS

There are many grants available, not only to support innovation but also to appraise various schemes and to encourage investment in the regions. The bank operates a comprehensive list of these grants and, again, can assist you with your applications.

5. CONCLUSION

It should be remembered that on the application for all loans and grants, the details discussed in this book will be necessary. The Appendices contain model applications which any bank would like to see.

6. INFORMATION THE BANK WILL REQUIRE

(i) What sort of loan do you require?
(ii) How much do you require?
(iii) For what purpose do you require the loan?
(iv) Over what period would you be able to repay?

CHAPTER EIGHT

TAXATION

1. INTRODUCTION

Whether the business initially makes a profit or not, it is essential that professional accounting advice is immediately sought. It is also necessary to notify the Inland Revenue that you have started a business - eventually, of course, you will be required to send in accounts so that your tax liability can be assessed. Needless to say, you will be expecting your business to make a profit, and this will give rise to a tax liability.

The rules for arriving at a net profit for tax purposes are extremely complex but, just as ignorance of the law is no excuse, so too there is no excuse for any business owner being unaware of his or her personal tax liability. Certainly, if the methods described in this book have been used, the proprietors will be aware of their likely profit as a result of their forecast. One of the advantages of knowing your likely profit is that you can plan your tax situation in order to obtain the maximum benefit from the tax legislation.

2. SOLE TRADER OR PARTNERSHIP

Both these types of business are taxed under Schedule D on the preceding year basis. Generally, no liability to tax can arise until at least twelve months' trading has occurred: it is then paid in the following year on the taxable profits, the first instalment being in January and the second in July. In arriving at taxable profit, all those allowable expenses which have arisen in running the business are deducted.

(i) Work in progress

It is unlikely that your business will be taxed on a cash basis as the Inland Revenue usually insists that all work in progress is taxed on its increased value each year. This is the normal basis. You can expect to be taxed on an earnings basis and freeze your work in progress. You will have to undertake not to withhold artificially your invoices at the year end, and will only pay tax on the invoices or fees actually achieved. The only difficulty with this is that, should the business change and give rise to what is known as "cessation", then the whole of the work in progress will be valued again and taxed accordingly.

(ii) Pensions

The bank can provide really comprehensive advice regarding pensions, which can be a very attractive way of saving money. An individual trader (or partner) can spend a considerable proportion of earnings on a pension and obtain full tax relief on it.

If, as in our example, the proprietor's profit is £9,279, then you could, at the present time, spend 17.5 per cent of that on pension - that is £1,624 per annum - and all the payment is allowable for tax at the highest rate. If you have been in business some time and never bought any pension, you can calculate the appropriate percentage for the previous six years and set all that payment off against your current tax liability.

(iii) Borrowings

Interest on any loans taken out by the proprietors to assist in running the business is also allowable against tax. When borrowing money from the bank, the level of taxation can affect the actual net cost. The types of loan available were discussed in the previous chapter.

3. COMPANIES

Although all companies have to pay corporation tax, there is what is known as a "small companies" rate which applies to those companies whose profits do not exceed a given figure, so you are well advised to seek proper accountancy advice. Similar allowances are available on expenditure too, as under

Schedule D, and tax is paid on the increased value of your stock from year to year.

Corporation tax is usually payable nine months after the accounting period for the company, and is assessed on the taxable profits. For this purpose these include an allowance for salaries for the directors. The directors pay tax under PAYE on such salaries in exactly the same way as employees. Any surplus funds in the business are usually distributed as remuneration though they can sometimes be more usefully paid by way of dividend. Either way, they are taxable once in the hands of the recipients.

(i) Dividend

A dividend is usually a payment made to shareholders in recognition of their stake in the company. A shareholder may be an individual (often a member of the family) or a company that has lent money to the business or, simply, a lender who insists on such a payment.

Where a dividend is paid, the liability to corporation tax is accelerated. Although the payment is subsequently allowed against the mainstream tax referred to above, payment in the first instance is usually made quarterly, fourteen days after the end of each return period.

(ii) Pensions

Again, the bank is able to advise on the complex provisions for the contributions made by the company to pensions for directors. Also worth considering is the establishment of the company's own, self-administered pension fund. This can be very attractive, as any payments made to such a fund are allowed against the profits of the company before tax.

4. ASSESSMENTS

The Inland Revenue's responsibility is to see that all tax due is paid - and paid on time. If an individual or a company fails to provide sufficient information for the Revenue to assess tax, then, in the absence of any reasonable excuse or explanation, the Revenue can raise an assessment by default. Many new and expanding businesses tend to be dilatory with their tax returns and we hope that this book has demonstrated the need to keep your financial affairs up-to-date.

Your accountant and, subsequently, the Inland Revenue will need information on your business's performance so that an assessment can be raised. When you receive your assessment, make sure your accountant is notified and deals with the matter. Failure to take such action can be extremely serious. First, the Revenue will apply to the General Commissioners for the Inland Revenue to have the assessment confirmed. Secondly, they can insist that accounts are produced and substantial penalties can be sought for failure to comply. Thirdly, if the accounts reveal a higher level of assessment, then additional tax can be levied. Unfortunately, if the accounts reveal a lower level of assessment - or even no tax liability at all - no refund is allowable.

In a properly organised business, utilising the principles suggested in this book, problems such as these should never arise.

CHAPTER NINE

MARKETING AND SELLING

1. DEFINITION

It is absolutely essential that you formulate a well-defined and structured marketing plan. Such a preparation is a vital part of the planning process which your business will need in order to grow and prosper. Marketing activity will be focused on identifying and satisfying the wants and needs of the business's actual and potential customers - at a worthwhile profit! It involves the promotion of your current product or service range, together with research into future developments which could be even more profitable and saleable.

Marketing provides the match which blends your business's financial, human and physical resources with your customers' needs and wants, and organises your operation in the direction of satisfying those needs.

The concept of the four Ps - Product, Price, Promotion and Place - is a useful starting point to begin any serious consideration of marketing. Thus, marketing addresses itself to the planning, co-ordination and control of the *product;* the *price* that is charged; the types of *promotion;* and the *places* where the product will be available or sold.

The blend of these four aspects is known as the marketing mix, and it is the responsibility of the marketing function to achieve a judicious and economical interaction of the elements to achieve success in the market place.

Of course, it is selling which is the specific task at the end of the marketing line; it can be described as getting the customer to want what your company has to offer. Advice on good sales techniques is given later in the chapter.

If the marketing side of the operation has been properly thought through, the selling will be made that much easier

- though, it must be said, never completely easy. If the marketing mix has not been properly planned, then all but the lucky can expect to fail! Good marketing will help you to avoid the common business error of not identifying the market properly, and thus failing to sell into it.

If your experience is biased to making and doing rather than marketing and selling, the thought of marketing may be intimidating. Remember that marketing is, by and large, a question of common sense. For example, can you give yourself positive answers to the following questions?

(i) Are you sure, before you commit money and effort, that what you are going to do will actually sell?

(ii) What is special or unique about your business and the products or services it offers?

Stop and think if your answers are vague or negative.

The rest of this chapter explains the four Ps in terms which you will need to relate to your own product or service.

2. PRODUCT (OR SERVICE)

Chapter Three will have helped you to decide and define exactly what benefits your product or service provides. Depending on its specification, this will encompass such things as: design, colour, finish, size range, packaging, quality standards, detailed description and specification of your service (and what it does not comprise), your terms and conditions, guarantees, after sales service, and policy regarding returned goods.

Additionally, you will need to assess the product potential - for example, can you see five years steady growth, followed by a decline? If so, can you envisage new or complementary products or services to keep your business growing? You will need to be in a favourable position to cope with these changed circumstances, and the earlier you begin the appropriate planning, the better placed you will be. Time and thought given to forward product or service plans can only be of assistance.

The following section describes how you should systematically set about conducting the product or service research which is such a vital part of the marketing mix.

(i) Market research

It is a common misconception to believe that market research ceases the moment your business starts to trade. In reality, it is essential to research your actual and potential markets continuously. This includes your customers, your competitors, suppliers, published information, trade associations and publications, small firms services, enterprise agencies and so on, all supplemented by your own intuitive feel for your market. Local further education establishments may also be seeking project work for their students.

Research is clearly more easily achieved if you are already running a going concern. But do not think you know it all! Significant new markets are often overlooked by existing established companies, with the result that newcomers arrive and take the opportunities from under their noses.

You will need to take your product or service idea and decide if there is a viable market for it, or for an improved variant. In either case you will need answers to the following questions:

(a) Who will use the proposed services or who will buy the proposed product (eg. younger men, women, shopkeepers, printers, families with young children and so on)?

(b) Why will they be interested enough to buy it?

(c) Where or how will they buy it?

(d) When, or in what circumstances, will they buy it?

(e) In what quantities will they buy it?

(f) Can it already be bought elsewhere?

A systematic assessment and honest, critical answers to such questions will help you to find an edge over your competition. Your particular selling proposition must be quickly and readily recognisable by your customers so that you can translate mere potential into good sales performance.

(ii) Practical ways to obtain information

(a) Customers

Your own customers are obviously the best people to tell you why they came to your business. You can use an unbiased questionnaire, but more practically do take the opportunity of talking to them personally. In fact, you should actively seek their observations not only on your business, but also on that of your competitors. You should constantly seek to identify your customers' changing needs so that you are well prepared to meet their future requirements.

(b) Suppliers

Do not forget that what you do with your customers, your suppliers are doing with theirs - they too have to anticipate market trends. Your time is at a premium, but discussions with your suppliers often spark off ideas which you may have been considering for some time.

(c) Journals, newspapers, etc.

All types of business have their own collection of trade magazines. It is impossible to read them all, but you should certainly study some of them. You should also read at least one quality newspaper.

Running your own business is undoubtedly about flair and imagination. Unless you have these qualities, your growth will be limited. Through trade magazines and through discussion and contact with your customers and suppliers you will be able to feed on the information made available.

(d) Trade fairs and conferences

It is often difficult to find time to attend trade fairs and conferences, and those which seem most appropriate may prove unsatisfactory. Their greatest strength is that they do get you out of your business, make you think objectively about your affairs, and sometimes provide a chance to see what the competition is up to.

(e) Competition

In any consideration of your market place, it is most important to take an objective view of your actual and potential competitors. Not only should you identify them with some care, but you should examine the way they operate in order to assess their strengths and weaknesses.

3. PRICE

This section describes in detail how you should go about the job of setting your prices. Before undertaking this task in detail, you must consider what the customer will pay and what prices your competitors are charging. If these are both less than you need to charge, then you should look again at your target market or your planned costings.

As explained earlier, running your own business must be about making a profit. In that context, a salary for yourself with a return on your capital employed is not truly profit. You will recall the example earlier:

	£	£
Expenses		10,000
Interest on capital	500	
Notional salary	12,500	
Contribution to pension	1,000	14,000
Required turnover		24,000

In real terms, £24,000 represents the minimum amount the business might reasonably expect to take before it starts to make any real profit. The additional profit (which is REAL profit) may be expressed as a percentage: as little as 5 per cent or as much as 25 per cent or, indeed, as much as the market will bear. Pricing decisions must therefore take these factors into account.

(i) Service industry

There is no doubt that the most effective means of assessing a price within the service industries is time. It is arguable that this can be used to good effect in manufacturing and retail businesses too. It is necessary to record time accurately, and for that purpose you will need to log this on a separate time sheet so that this can be collated, either daily or weekly, and carried to an appropriate work sheet for each client. At the conclusion of the work (or on an interim basis) the client will be charged for the time at the agreed rate.

In Figure 3 you can see that the total expenses forecast for the present year are £42,655. This includes £5,000 as salaries for the proprietor, but there needs to be added interest on capital employed and a contribution to a pension. The figures might appear as follows:

	£
Expenses	42,655
Return on capital	480
17.5% of say £14,000	2,450
Real costs	45,585

Chapter Eight, which dealt with taxation and pensions, explained the reference to 17.5 per cent. It is assumed for the purposes of this book that in addition to the owner, there are three other people actively involved in the business. If those individuals work 1,500 hours every year then, at best, 1,000 of those hours are expended servicing clients. It is then possible to calculate how much time each must charge for every hour worked in order to cover the real costs of £45,585 It should also be noted that if 25 per cent (as your profit percentage) is added to £45,585 then a turnover of £52,423 will be achieved.

Interestingly enough, the forecast prepared in Figure 4 produces a very similar figure - namely £51,934. This is not surprising, and if there is a big discrepancy then both sets of figures should be recalculated. As the figures *are* much the same, it is possible to calculate the hourly rate which each productive member of staff must charge simply by using their forecast figures in Figure 4.

First take the forecast figure. Then calculate the basic figure to which the real profit of 25 per cent must be added in order to produce the forecast figure. In the case of the owner in the calculation on the next page, £20,424. If he works productively for 1,000 hours, he will have to charge £20 for every hour worked in order to cover the real expenses of £20,424 needed to run the business.

Calculation of Time Charge

	Forecast	Figure to which 25% is added to achieve forecast	Divide by hours worked	Expense rate per hour
	£	£		£
Owner	25,530	20,424	1,000	20
Manager	19,425	15,540	1,000	16
Staff 1	4,729	3,783	1,000	4
Staff 2	2,250	1,800	1,000	2
	51,934	41,547		

The manager has to carry out work which will command an expense rate of £16 per hour. If the manager adds up all the time spent on any client, and then multiplies it by the expense rate of £16, this will be the minimum that the business ought to charge in order to cover the real costs. It is also hoped, of course, that an additional 25 per cent can be added, though sometimes this may be less or more, depending on the circumstances. In any event, it is essential to ensure that your charges are in line with your competitors.

(ii) Manufacturing and retail business

It should be possible to cost out the price of individual products by using a similar system to that discussed above. It is common, however, for a price to be struck in relation to the volume of the particular product - after allocating an appropriate share of overhead, plus a profit mark-up. Again, it is essential that your product sells at the appropriate price in the market place. The price would be calculated as follows:

(a) Value of stock/or raw material

plus

(b) Expenses as discussed above, including the appropriate additions and the manufacturing costs and other overheads

plus

(c) A percentage mark-up of between 5 per cent and 25 per cent.

If you have just one product, you would need only to divide the number of items into this total cost. You might divide them into the appropriate cost prior to the addition of the percentage mark-up, which would leave you a facility to vary the price according not only to current market price, but also to the achievements of your own business. It would also give you the price below which you could not go if you were to remain viable.

(iii) Long term building contract price

From what has been discussed already, it can be seen that the most effective type of pricing structure is the one which matches the right amount of overhead to the right contract. In a contract which might run for some time, this relationship may be critical. In most building contracts, the materials are usually readily identifiable and the overheads can also be allocated to the appropriate contract. In simple terms: if there are five equal contracts requiring an equal amount of labour, then each will carry 1/5th of the overhead. For example:

	£
Materials	15,000
Direct wages and salaries over three months	9,900
Proportion of total overheads	20,800

This would mean that the direct overhead (£20,800) represented 210 per cent of the (£9,900) wages. To fine tune the contract as you go along, you can apply this percentage each month to the actual wages paid in order to see whether you are achieving your forecast. If your percentage overhead fails to cover your anticipated overhead, then clearly your profit margin will be less.

(iv) VAT

If the turnover is above the minimum limit for registration purposes, then VAT will have to be added. This might take your price structure over the market price. In those circumstances you may have to look again at your pricing structure.

(v) Marginal cost

As you will now be operating to a forecast, you will be able to fine tune your prices accordingly. If you anticipate achieving your forecast result, then it may be possible to reduce your prices to put pressure on your competitors. Even if you have not achieved your target, you may still be able to reduce price, because the particular income will be making a contribution to your overhead. The argument is that you have a fixed overhead cost, and you are better to have a contract that makes a contribution to that expense than do nothing. If you price all your business on this latter basis, you will, of course, be in grave difficulties. But you should have sufficient information to know exactly what your position is, and so you will be able to price your product or service accordingly.

4. PROMOTION

This heading comprises the wide array of promotional methods available, including advertising, brochures, sales promotion tools such as competitions and give-aways, telephone selling, press, TV and radio coverage, posters and personal selling.

You must remember that not all these will be effective or even viable in your own particular context. The fundamental requirement of each item is that it communicates your required message to the appropriate target audience at the optimum cost. The communication should then persuade enough people to buy your product or use your service. No promotional effort has any value if it fails to increase sales or customers.

It is perhaps appropriate to deal first with those techniques of personal selling which are particularly important in industry and retail/wholesale outlets.

You should remember, though, that in the communications mix, as in the marketing mix as a whole, you must select the basic elements in order to achieve the goals which you have already set. Also, bear in mind that your customers only see what you put before them and they see it with *their* eyes, not yours!

Personal calling is less likely to work without a prior appointment. The telephone can be a very potent tool: use it to inform your prospective clients or customers that you will be in the area in the next few days, and ask if it would be convenient to call. You should be able to find out what you need from the "what for?" which follows. This is the way into the market place; how to make the sale follows.

(i) Personal calling - customer contact

The most difficult part of any business, and particularly a new business, is securing your first sale. If you have acquired an existing business you will have an existing clientele - one which you will at least have the opportunity of keeping and building upon.

Starting from scratch is very much harder. First you must make sure that the person you are talking to has the authority to complete the contract with you. If not, you should try to bring in the person who does have that authority. This is not always easy, and often you will have to make a judgment for yourself when speaking to the individual concerned.

Always be sure to arrive on time if possible, even a little early. This will give you the chance to compose yourself and attempt to get a feel for the business you are visiting. Try to appear friendly: smile when you can, and aim to get a two-way conversation going as soon as possible, even if that conversation has little or nothing to do with your visit.

Once on to your subject, stress the positive virtues and benefits of what you are selling to this business. Simply asking if the potential customer requires two gross of widgets provides an easy way of saying "No thank you."

When objections are raised, listen without interrupting and try to explore the merits of the point without arguing. "It's too expensive" may mean he has a cash flow problem. Find helpful ways around objections.

If you have a sample or samples, be sure to take them with you - otherwise there is not much point in you having them at all. If your samples are too big, then have a brochure available . . . and possibly supporting visual aids too. Have a notepad, pen and your visiting card to hand and remember that you have every confidence in your product, so be positive.

People do not generally like to be rude, especially if they have gone out of their way to see you. So, when discussing the product with the potential customer, listen to what they are saying. It may be that your product is not what they have in mind. If you do not secure a sale, it does no harm to suggest somewhere they might be able to get what they are looking for. They will remember you as being helpful and having integrity - two key points to encourage them to recommend you to someone else.

(ii) Closing the sale

If the interview is going well, you need to judge when it would be appropriate to encourage the customer or client to make an order. Easier said than done, as this is a particularly difficult thing to gauge - but you will improve with experience. Questions such as "How soon can you deliver?" or "What are your trade terms?" are likely clues.

Remember: your objective is to close the sale and, eventually, you are going to have to ask them to place an order and to pay your price. You should therefore lead them to that position by asking how many of your products they would like and, ultimately, getting them to sign an order form. If they cannot make a decision immediately, arrange to leave them something which you will have to call back for - your only sample (even if it isn't). And if you do have to go back, follow the sale up quickly.

There are alternative sale-closing techniques which avoid the yes/no crunch and they are worth remembering or using. The "alternative close" and the "assumed close" are two examples. The first assumes a "yes" answer and leapfrogs it. Simply ask if the customer would prefer delivery on Monday or Wednesday, or some similar type of alternative. In answering your question, your prospect will have committed himself.

The "assumed close" is exactly what it says it is - an assumption that your prospect has decided to buy. The technique is to say something like "If you initial this order note, we will deliver within seven days." You have effectively made the decision for the customer. If this does not work straight away, ie. if the customer says "Hang on, I haven't decided to buy yet", you could reply "Sorry, I thought you had. Are there any further matters you need clearing up before signing?" This still suggests an eventual order by implying that, in your opinion, logic and common sense dictate that once you have answered the next question, then the order should be forthcoming.

If you are selling from your premises remember the customer is always right. Never be discourteous - even if you feel exasperated. You will not only fail to secure a sale but, more importantly, you will also have an individual who will go out of his or her way to discourage others from coming to you. It is not possible, of course, to please everybody, and there are some people who will make sure that you cannot!

Perhaps it would be a good idea to go shopping yourself and see what sort of service YOU like best and why. If you are selling goods in a shop, try to be interested in what the customer wants. Introduce items to them rather than merely asking if you can help - of course you can, otherwise you would not be there. How many times have you been in a shop where the sales assistants lounged around away from the serving area discussing television while you tried to find a particular item?

Selling is a topic on its own, but once you have secured one or two sales you will be well on the way to success.

(iii) Advertising and other media

This section covers advertising and other promotional techniques, such as press releases and corporate design. In contrast with the last section, they are mainly impersonal means of stimulating sales.

(a) Legal constraints

Before you do - or even consider doing - anything within the advertising sphere, it is appropriate here to note that you should be mindful of the legal considerations involved in planning the promotion of your business.

You need to consider legal, professional and trade restrictions. Professional services have substantial constraints which limit the types of permitted marketing activity. This may not be as true in manufacturing or retail businesses, but care should be taken to ensure that you do not infringe the trade marks or copyright of another company. The Advertising Standards Authority (ASA) rubric "legal, decent, honest and truthful" is useful to bear in mind when considering advertising copy. The Trade Descriptions Act makes it an offence to apply a false description to goods or services, and you often find that the local authority trading standards officers are vigilant in enforcing good trading practices.

(b) Design of your business name and letterheads

Your initial requirement is, of course, the printed material (letterheads, business cards, etc.) on which, with which and from which you conduct your business affairs. Unless your business is of the type which traditionally trades under the name of the partner or partners (eg. accountants, dentists, etc.), do not pass lightly over the opportunity of trading under a business name. A well chosen name can convey a sales message to your customer, and is therefore a useful promotional tool. And if you have a good idea for a company logo, use it.

It is also worthwhile to decide on a standardised corporate identity. This means that you should select and use standard typefaces, colours and designs. Your letterhead and business cards should be of the same basic design and may include an appropriate sales message. Do not forget to include post code and STD code - and mention if you have an answering service or a fax number. Letters are normally A4 size and business cards about 9 cm. x 5.5cm., and any design features should be carried through to invoices, advertising, brochures and so on.

You should also ensure that you include the business address and the name of the sole trader or all partners on your letterheaded paper. Limited companies must show the full company name, country of registration (eg. England, Wales, etc.) and the registration number. If you wish to show the names of *any* director then *all* must be shown.

(c) Advertising and design

Advertising is only of any value if it increases customers or if it sells to existing customers. It is therefore necessary to decide upon a budget and to monitor the results to ensure that the expenditure is justified.

Do not think that you can create good advertising effortlessly. In fact, even seemingly simple classified advertising follows basic rules, and all advertising tries to target the message towards readers who will actually buy the advertised product or service.

In designing the advertisement, remember that you are trying to arouse the interest of specific readers, and to encourage them to take the next step - in other words, you want them to send for a brochure, send money or perhaps visit your premises.

Classified advertising will benefit from a witty or catchy heading. Two or more shorter advertisements in the same issue are likely to be more effective than one long one. You should also consider coding your address for orders and inquiries (eg. Dept. G) so that you can monitor to which advert your inquirer responded.

Display advertising benefits from a well chosen photograph or a sketch, but do not be tempted to fill all the space with extraneous clutter! Remember that the purpose of the advertisement is to promote action from readers.

When in doubt, the professional advice of a good local advertising agency can be invaluable, although you must take care this does not become too expensive in relation to your total advertising budget.

(d) Publications

You will probably have a reasonable idea which publications are likely to fulfil your needs as to target market, specialised readership, and so on. Your local library should have the current copy of BRAD (British Rates and Data), which gives all the technical and other details - costs, copy dates, circulation, contact addresses - for all publications which carry advertising and circulate in the United Kingdom. Similar details are provided for commercial television and radio.

(e) Freepost

The freepost or business reply paid services offered by the Post Office are well worth considering if you wish to encourage a greater response to your advertising. They mean that potential customers can write to you at no cost to themselves and avoid the physical trouble of actually buying stamps. The Post Office is keen to encourage new users of these services and frequently offers special terms to first time users. Local contacts can be found in the telephone directory.

(f) Brochures and leaflets

The main purpose of a leaflet is to convey your message in a more lasting form than used within an advertisement. Of course, in general terms, a leaflet can also carry a much larger message than an advertisement. But you will need to consider the following points:

> DESIGN: Professional help will present your leaflet in a way to gain maximum effect. CONTENT: An effective leaflet has some of the characteristics of a letter but, more specifically, the HEADING will focus the reader's mind on your offer, and draw attention to your product and to its benefits; the INTRODUCTION, normally a short paragraph, will explain and expand on the heading; the MAIN BODY, which can be up to several paragraphs in length, explains your product or service offer; and the ACTION you wish the reader to take (contact by phone or

letter, or a simple reply coupon may be useful). This should always be at the end of the leaflet.

Additionally, you will need to think about size. Variations on the A4 format are most commonly used for leaflets. Consider whether your leaflet should be printed on both sides, and whether to go for flat or folded. Your intended method of distribution - eg. post, door-to-door drop, newspaper or magazine insert - will influence your choice.

It is expensive to produce full colour leaflets and you should be sure that the expense is justified, either to show the product features or to meet competition which uses this method. If colour is not essential, effective results can be obtained by using two or three colour printing.

The essential thing to remember is that the leaflet or brochure will reflect *your* business and *your* products or services, so however much or little you spend, do avoid anything that looks cheap or tatty.

(g) Press releases

Editorial coverage is a valuable promotional bonus for your business. It is not difficult to achieve if you set about the task in a professional manner. Press releases should be sent to all relevant publications whenever you have something which is newsworthy. Include good quality black and white photographs, preferably featuring people. You should put a description of what the photo shows, plus the names of the people pictured, on the reverse. Quotes from relevant people, such as the local enterprise agency or your bank manager, are useful. You should not make suspect claims or use too many superlatives. Similar techniques can be employed with other media, particularly local radio.

(h) Further methods

There is a wide range of other promotion methods which may be appropriate to your business. These include:

- Promotional giveaways with your company name - pens, desk sets, diaries, etc.
- Free samples.

- Special discounts (eg. to students or pensioners).
- Competitions.
- Mail shots using your brochure, or your own magazine, if you have the money.

5. PLACE

Businesses frequently concentrate on the first three elements of the marketing mix while neglecting the practicalities of "place".

Clearly the concept of place can have different meanings, depending on the type of business which you are running. In retailing, it is largely the shop or shops which form your business, while in manufacturing it refers mainly to the distribution function.

Welding place into your business plans involves considering the following questions:

Will you be involved in direct sales (eg. mail order)?

Will you sell direct to shops or through mail order?

Do you need an expensive high street location?

Do you need street level access?

Should you lease or buy premises?

Will you need to appoint agents?

How many staff will you need to employ?

What opening hours should you offer?

What types of outlet will you concentrate on?

What are the implications of this in terms of distribution costs and vehicle requirements?

What sort of stock levels are required at each outlet?

How often will each need visiting?

Remember that this activity is necessary to ensure that the right product service is available in the right place at the right time. Considerations such as those mentioned above are marketing channels, which can best be described as the route taken in the movement of a product or service from its original source of supply to its point of consumption or use.

Bear in mind that many products require an ongoing after-sales service which can not only generate revenue in its own right (sometimes more, over a period of time, than the original sale), but also lead to further repeat business.

Many businesses fail to pay much attention to the question of distribution channels. They therefore tend to develop in an unplanned and haphazard way which will tend to undermine customer confidence if customers cannot rely on the continuity of stock or service levels. Never forget: customers vote with their feet - they can usually take their custom elsewhere.

On the other hand, it may be that your business only requires an address and telephone number, so your own home would be eminently suitable. If it is not necessary to have either prestigious - or indeed any! - office accommodation, then there is little point in wasting money on premises. The resources saved would undoubtedly be better deployed in a bigger advertising budget or in newer and more reliable vehicles.

6. CONCLUSION

The purpose of the four Ps in the marketing mix is, of course, to create an awareness of your product or service. Until people know about you, they cannot make any decision to use you. However, once their interest has been captured you have started the process which leads your prospect to take some direct action to buy your product or use your service.

Finally, remember that customers need changeover time. A thorough review is required, not only when starting a business, but also an appraisal of the marketing mix at regular intervals to adapt to changing circumstances.

7. INFORMATION THE BANK WILL REQUIRE

(i) How are your prices càlculated and reviewed?
(ii) Are your products or services sensitive to price?
(iii) How do your products compare with those of your competitors?
(iv) Have you samples or a brochure?
(v) Have you a thorough knowledge of your actual and your potential markets?

APPENDIX A

SERVICE INDUSTRY MODEL:
Application for a Loan

BACKGROUND

William Green, of 5 Somerton Road, Anytown, is 32 and married with a son. He was educated at Edgeworth Secondary Modern School and left at 16. He originally worked in a small business as an office boy, but subsequently moved to a larger concern, where he was in charge of a team supervising safety standards and hygiene. He received a salary of £9,500, and a pension of two thirds of his final salary was anticipated on his retirement. Three years ago he started a small office contract cleaning business with his wife and now he wishes to expand the business, although competition in the area has become more fierce in the meantime.

PROPOSAL

For the past three years we have been operating an office contract cleaning business for industry, business, offices and homes. During this time we have gained considerable practical experience. There is one large cleaning contractor in the immediate vicinity, but they appear to be involved with British Rail and one other major customer. The economy in the town has picked up quite markedly. Our existing customers are listed at the end of this note. Our research and experience shows that there is scope for further growth during the next 12 months, and to take advantage of this we need new vehicles and cleaning equipment.

We employ some 50 middle-aged ladies who work for two hours on three nights a week, and we believe we can contain their wages to £19,000 for the coming year. We appreciate that they require substantial supervision, which we consider critical to maintaining the quality of cleaning that our customers will expect.

FIGURES

There is attached to this note our projection of the expenses for the next twelve months (Figure 3), with a build up of income over the same period (Figure 7). You will note that we anticipate the first few months will be slow. Our solicitors are Williams and Co. of Nelson Street, Anytown (D. Williams) and our accountants are Drifford and Co., of 20 Print Street, Anytown (M.W. Drifford).

CASH FLOW

The cash flow projection (Figure 10) shows that we will need an overdraft facility of £4,541 in September. The position should improve by April next year. The need for the increased overdraft is principally because we have been forced to change the terms of trade to our customers to retain business as a result of competition.

SECURITY

We own our house which is now worth £40,000 with a mortgage of £20,000. We could put the house up as security.

EXISTING CUSTOMERS

Wigglesworth & Co. Limited	Williamson and Co.	Theatre Unlimited
Bloomers Limited	Snook Frodsham	Parish Church
E.K.G. & Co.	Oval and Round	Dancing and Co.
Mistry and Company	Omega Limited	Rogers and Green
Jones (Shoes) Limited	Smith and Weston	Overland Travel
Hudson's	Patel and Co.	Clik's Jewellers
Browns	Ready Print	Metcalfe and Co.
Fleet Hire Limited	Leyland Vehicles	Subaqua Limited
Atlas and Company	Open Air Shows	McGills Insurance

NOTE

This application to the bank should be accompanied by Figures 3, 6, 7, 10 and 11 shown on the following pages.

SERVICE INDUSTRY MODEL:
Management Figures

FIGURE 1: PROFIT & LOSS ACCOUNT

	Year 1 £		Year 2 £	% turnover
Income	43322	Fees (see Fig 2)	46787	100
Wages	16509	Wages	17500	
	4750	Drawings	5000	
	21259	Total	22500	48
Office Expenses	532	Books	564	
	2115	Photocopying	472	
	928	Postages	984	
	1260	Telephone	1336	
	641	Stationery	680	
	1698	Cars	1800	
	450	Typewriters	500	
	7624	Total	6336	14
Building Expenses	2750	Rent	2750	
	583	Rates	688	
	162	Electricity	176	
	120	Gas	130	
	296	Repairs	320	
	3911	Total	4064	9
Finance	266	Bank Interest	350	
	10	Donations	15	
	245	Insurance	275	
	650	Auditors	750	
	1075	Advertising	1150	
	1328	Depreciation	1395	
	3574	Total	3935	8
Miscellaneous	75	Courses	85	
	300	Entertainment	225	
	228	Parking	300	
	500	Staff Adverts	360	
	85	Newspapers	125	
	1637	Sundries	1965	
	2825	Total	3060	6
	39193	TOTAL EXPENSES	39895	85
	4129	PROFIT BEFORE TAX	6892	15

FIGURE 2: ANALYSIS OF TURNOVER

	Product	Amount Invoiced £	Core Total £	%
Core Group 1	A	4610		
	B	6442		
	C	3608		
	D	1980		
	E	2075	18715	40
Core Group 2	F	7298		
	G	3270		
	H	2806		
	I	3000	16374	35
Core Group 3	J	3808		
	K	1483		
	L	791	6082	13
Core Group 4	M	3167		
	N	882	4049	9
Miscellaneous	O	1567	1567	3
TOTAL			46787	100

New

Department	A	B	C	D	E	F	G	H	I	J	K	L	M	N	O	Totals
1	✓✓	✓✓✓✓✓			✓✓✓											0
2	✓	✓✓✓✓	✓✓✓	✓✓	✓✓											0
3						✓✓	✓	✓✓✓✓	✓✓✓✓							0
4			✓			✓✓✓	✓✓	✓✓✓	✓✓✓✓✓	✓✓	✓	✓				0
5										✓	✓✓✓	✓	✓		✓✓✓	0
Totals	0	0	0	0	0	0	0	0	0	0	0	0	0	0	0	0

Invoiced

Department	A	B	C	D	E	F	G	H	I	J	K	L	M	N	O	Totals
1	2	8			5											15
2	1	5	3	2	2											13
3						2	1	4	7							14
4			1			3	2	3	4	8	2	1	1			25
5										1	3	1	1		4	10
Totals	3	13	4	2	7	5	3	7	11	9	5	2	2	0	4	77

FIGURE 3: FORECAST OF EXPENSES

		Last Year £	% Rise	Forecast £
Income	Fees (see Fig 2)	46787	11	51934
Wages	Wages	17500	9	19075
	Drawings	5000	9	5450
	Total..................	22500	9	24525
Office	Books	564	5	592
Expenses	Photocopying	472	5	496
	Postages	984	5	1033
	Telephone	1336	5	1403
	Stationery	680	5	714
	Cars	1800	5	1890
	Typewriters	500	5	525
	Total..................	6336	5	6653
Building	Rent	2750	0	2750
Expenses	Rates	688	5	722
	Electricity	176	5	185
	Gas	130	5	137
	Repairs	320	5	336
	Total..................	4064		4130
Finance	Bank Interest	350	5	368
	Donations	15	5	16
	Insurance	275	5	289
	Auditors	750	5	788
	Advertising	1150	5	1208
	Depreciation	1395	–	1465
	Total..................	3935	5	4134
Misc.	Course	85	5	89
	Entertainment	225	5	236
	Sundries	2750	5	2888
	Total..................	3060	5	3213
	TOTAL EXPENSES	39895		42655
	PROFIT BEFORE TAX	6892		9279

FIGURE 4: FORECAST ANALYSIS OF TURNOVER

	Last Year £	% Rise	Forecast £
Sales Mix			
Core Group 1	18715	10.5	20672
Core Group 2	16374	12.0	18339
Core Group 3	6082	10.0	6690
Core Group 4	4049	11.0	4494
Core Group 5	1567	11.0	1739
Total.................	46787		51934
Productive Staff			
Owner	23000		25530
Manager 1	17500		19425
Staff 1	4287		4759
Staff 2	2000		2220
Total.................	46787		51934

To calculate the forecast for the productive staff, multiply the previous year's figures by 51934/46787.

FIGURE 5: FIVE YEAR PLAN

	Year 1 £	%	Year 2 £	%	Year 3 £	%	Year 4 £	%	Year 5 £
SALES									
Core 1	20672	9	22532	7	24110	5	25315	3	26075
Core 2	18339	10	20173	8	21787	12	24401	13	27573
Core 3	6690	8	7225	8	7803	10	8584	11	9528
Core 4	4494	6	4764	6	5049	9	5504	10	6054
Core 5	1739	8	1878	8	2028	8	2191	8	2366
Total.........	51934		56572		60778		65994		71596
EXPENSES									
Wages	24525	9	26732	9	29138	6	30886	9	33666
Office	6653	10	7318	10	8050	6	8533	6	9045
Building	4130	6	4378	6	4640	6	4919	6	5214
Finance	4134	6	4382	6	4645	6	4924	6	5219
Misc.	3213	6	3406	6	3610	6	3827	6	4056
Total.........	42655		46216		50083		53089		57200
Net Profit	9279		10356		10695		12905		14396
% of Sales	18		18		18		20		20

FIGURE 6: BUDGET EXPENSES

		Budget	May	June	July	1/4	Aug	Sep
		£	£	£	£	£	£	£
Wages	Wages	19075	1796	1437	1437	4670	1437	1437
	Drawings	5450	524	419	524	1467	419	419
	Total	24525	2320	1856	1961	6137	1856	1856
Office	Books	592	53	49	49	151	49	49
	Photocopying	496	41	41	41	123	41	41
	Postages	1033	86	86	86	258	86	86
	Telephone	1403	0	0	351	351	0	0
	Stationery	714	179	0	0	179	179	0
	Cars	1890	478	128	128	734	128	128
	Typewriters	525	459	0	0	459	0	0
	Total	6653	1296	304	655	2255	483	304
Building	Rent	2750	0	688	0	688	0	687
	Rates	722	60	60	60	180	60	60
	Electricity	185	0	0	46	46	0	0
	Gas	137	0	0	34	34	0	0
	Repairs	336	0	0	0	0	0	168
	Total	4130	60	748	140	948	60	915
Finance	Bank Interest	368	0	92	0	92	0	92
	Donations	16	0	0	0	0	0	0
	Insurance	289	24	24	24	72	24	24
	Auditors	788	197	0	0	197	197	0
	Advertising	1208	101	101	101	303	101	101
	Depreciation	1465	0	0	0	0	0	0
	Total	4134	322	217	125	664	322	217
Misc.	Courses	89	0	0	45	45	0	0
	Entertainment	236	118	0	0	118	0	0
	Sundries	3008	278	222	278	778	222	222
	Total	3213	396	222	323	941	222	222
TOTAL EXPENSES		42655	4394	3347	3204	10945	2943	3514

FIGURE 7: BUDGET TURNOVER

	Budget	May	June	July	1/4	Aug	Sep
	£	£	£	£	£	£	£
Core Group 1	20672	1100	1300	1700	4100	1200	1200
Core Group 2	18339	1200	1100	1225	3525	1100	1100
Core Group 3	6690	275	360	425	1060	590	375
Core Group 4	4494	275	325	250	850	305	375
Core Group 5	1739	100	125	190	415	175	168
Total	51934	2950	3210	3790	9950	3370	3218

1/2	Nov	Dec	Jan	3/4	Feb	Mar	Apr	TOTAL
£	£	£	£	£	£	£	£	£
9340	1437	2191	1796	14764	1437	1437	1437	19075
2829	419	419	524	4191	419	419	421	5450
2169	1856	2610	2320	18955	1856	1856	1858	24525
298	49	49	49	445	49	49	49	592
246	41	41	41	369	41	41	45	496
516	86	86	86	774	86	87	86	1033
702	0	0	351	1053	0	0	350	1403
358	0	250	0	608	0	0	106	714
1118	128	128	128	1502	128	128	132	1890
459	0	0	66	525	0	0	0	525
3697	304	554	721	5276	304	305	768	6653
1375	0	688	0	2063	0	687	0	2750
360	60	60	60	540	60	60	62	722
92	0	0	46	138	0	0	47	185
68	0	0	34	102	0	0	35	137
168	0	0	0	168	0	168	0	336
2063	60	748	140	3011	60	915	144	4130
184	0	92	0	276	0	92	0	368
0	0	16	0	16	0	0	0	16
144	24	24	24	216	24	24	25	289
394	197	0	0	591	197	0	0	788
606	101	101	101	909	101	97	101	1208
0	0	0	0	0	0	0	1465	1465
1328	322	233	125	2008	322	213	1591	4134
45	0	0	0	45	44	0	0	89
118	0	118	0	236	0	0	0	236
1500	222	222	278	2222	222	222	222	2888
1663	222	340	278	2503	266	222	222	3213
1920	2764	4485	3584	31753	2808	3511	4583	42655

1/2	Nov	Dec	Jan	3/4	Feb	Mar	Apr	TOTAL
£	£	£	£	£	£	£	£	£
5150	2250	1300	2250	13950	2250	2150	2322	20672
5725	1528	1200	2200	11653	1975	2514	2197	18339
2445	575	475	875	4370	760	975	585	6690
2180	310	275	475	3240	375	508	371	4494
893	125	110	130	1258	154	162	165	1739
9393	4788	3360	5930	34471	5514	6309	5640	51934

FIGURE 8: ANALYSING PERFORMANCE

	A Annual Budget £	B Actual May £	C Budget June £	D Actual June £	E Variance June (D−C) £	F Year To Date (B+D) £
INCOME						
Core Group 1	20672	1100	1300	1125	−175	2225
Core Group 2	18339	1200	1100	975	−125	2175
Core Group 3	6690	275	360	420	60	695
Core Group 4	4494	275	325	300	−25	575
Core Group 5	1739	100	125	118	−7	218
Total	51934	2950	3210	2938	−272	5888
EXPENSES						
Wages	24525	2320	1856	1856	0	4176
Office	6653	1296	304	400	96	1696
Building	4130	60	748	725	−23	785
Finance	4134	322	217	200	−17	522
Misc.	3213	396	222	210	−12	606
Total	42655	4394	3347	3391	44	7785
GROSS PROFIT	9279	−1444	−137	−453	−316	−1897

FIGURE 9: QUARTERLY PROFIT & LOSS

		Budget £	Actual £	Variance £
Income	Core Group 1	4100	4250	150
	Core Group 2	3525	3750	225
	Core Group 3	1060	1200	140
	Core Group 4	850	765	−85
	Core Group 5	415	387	−28
	Total	9950	10352	402
Expenses				
Wages	Wages	4670	4670	0
	Drawings	1467	1467	0
	Total	6137	6137	0
Office	Books	151	75	−76
	Photocopying	123	125	2
	Postages	258	275	17
	Telephone	351	345	−6
	Stationery	179	160	−19
	Cars	734	825	91
	Typewriters	459	459	0
	Total	2255	2264	9
Building	Rent	688	688	0
	Rates	180	180	0
	Electricity	46	47	1
	Gas	34	38	4
	Repairs	0	15	15
	Total	948	968	20
Finance	Bank Interest	92	92	0
	Donations	0	0	0
	Insurance	72	89	17
	Auditors	197	197	0
	Advertising	303	275	−28
	Depreciation	0	0	0
	Total	664	653	−11
Misc.	Courses	45	34	−11
	Entertainment	118	165	47
	Sundry	778	756	−22
	Total	941	955	14
	TOTAL EXPENSES	10945	10977	32
	PROFIT BEFORE TAX	−995	−625	370

FIGURE 10: CASH FLOW

	May £	June £	Jul £	Aug £	Sep £	Oc £
INCOME						
Debtors/Cash Sale	2478	2696	3184	2830	2703	323
VAT received	438	475	562	503	477	57
Capital Introduced	0	0	0	0	0	
Other Cash	440	472	560	525	475	57
Bank Loan	4250	0	0	0	0	
Total .... (A)	7606	3643	4306	3858	3655	438
PAYMENTS						
Expenses	3870	2928	2680	2524	3095	299
Drawings	375	375	375	375	375	37
Loan Repayment	0	120	120	120	120	12
VAT	0	1344	0	0	1557	
Tax	0	0	506	0	0	
Capital items	4250	0	0	0	0	
Total .... (B)	8495	4767	3681	3019	5147	348
CASH FLOW (A−B)	−889	−1124	625	839	−1492	89
BANK BALANCE b/f	−2500	−3389	−4513	−3888	−3049	−454
BANK BALANCE c/f	−3389	−4513	−3888	−3049	−4541	−364

	Nov	Dec	Jan	Feb	Mar	Apr
	£	£	£	£	£	£
	4022	2824	4981	4632	5299	4738
	717	496	878	823	941	844
	0	0	0	500	0	0
	755	485	875	855	975	890
	0	0	0	0	0	0
	5494	3805	6734	6810	7215	6472
	2345	4066	3061	2389	3092	2697
	375	375	375	375	375	375
	120	120	120	120	120	120
	0	1800	0	0	2663	0
	0	0	506	0	0	0
	0	0	0	0	0	0
	2840	6361	4062	2884	6250	3192
	2654	−2556	2672	3926	965	3280
	−3644	−990	−3546	−874	3052	4017
	−990	−3546	−874	3052	4017	7297

FIGURE 11: PROJECTED BALANCE SHEET as at 30 April 19--

	£	£	£
CAPITAL ACCOUNT			
Capital b/f		12862	
Funds introduced		500	
Interest on capital		60	
Profit (as forecast Fig 3)		9219	
Total		22641	
Less -			
Drawings	4500		
Tax	1012	5512	
CAPITAL c/f			17129
Fixed Assets			
Lease (at Valuation)	2750		
Less Depreciation	550	2200	
Machinery/Office equipment	1980		
Less Depreciation	396	1584	
Vehicles	2595		
Less Depreciation	519	2076	
TOTAL FIXED ASSETS			5860
Current Assets			
Work in progress		4535	
Debtors		5238	
Cash at Bank		7297	
Total		17070	
Current Liabilities			
Creditors		2365	
Tax		506	
Bank overdraft		0	
Bank loan		2930	
Total		5801	
NET CURRENT ASSETS			11269
TOTAL ASSETS			17129

APPENDIX B

MANUFACTURING INDUSTRY MODEL:
Application for a Loan

BACKGROUND

Fred Lomax, of 9 The Mews, Anytown, is 35 and married with two children. He has, until recently, been involved at club level with a local judo team. He was educated at Southworth Secondary School, and took a foundation course at the local technical college.

He was working for a small textile company in their production department on an annual wage of £8,500. A pension of two thirds his final salary was anticipated on his retirement. He had £500 of ready cash to hand. While working in the production department, he had been responsible for three men, and had to organise his time efficiently and without supervision. He had no time off work and, apart from the usual colds, has enjoyed good health.

Fred decided to set up his own business manufacturing a new type of judo uniform. His manager is John Wilson, of 42 The Terraces, Anytown, who is 32 and single. He is interested in squash, tennis and weight training. He too was educated at Southworth Secondary School, and went on to the local college to study business administration. He worked as a cashier at a local health club on a wage of £5,500, but was not entitled to a pension.

While working at the health club he was in complete charge of the office, as the owner had left him to run the administrative side of the business for him. He enjoys excellent health.

PRODUCT

Fred discovered that he could manufacture a judo uniform which is both tougher and more durable than some of the foreign products currently available. Fred's wife made some uniforms, which stood up well and were widely admired. As a result, some two dozen suits were made for friends and for people they had recommended.

Fred left his job and started his company. Originally he worked from home, but recently increased his stock of cloth. Where possible the customer was asked to pay half the price with the order, and the balance on completion. Fred is dealing principally with the local judo clubs.

There was no resistance to the company's pricing structure as there was no competition locally for the suits.

After a short time Fred moved the operation out of his house and into a small enterprise unit. He also bought three sewing machines with "twin needles" which helped to speed up the process considerably. Two girls were employed to sew, and Mrs Lomax was placed in charge of production.

The company organised its own labels, designed in-house, to make the suits distinctive. Customers and sources of raw material were identified and the company obtained the services of a self-employed sales representative, whom Fred knew, to sell the product in the region. Nationwide expansion has been planned.

SALES POTENTIAL

There are many thousands of judo, wrestling and similar clubs in Britain and these provide the company with a large potential market. Before the sales rep started, the company was taking about 26 orders a week for a suit which sells at £65.

ACCOUNTS

A copy of the forecast for next year is attached. The figures are obtained from a standard book keeping system on a manual basis. John Wilson has some experience in working a spread sheet, but they feel the business is not yet large enough to warrant full computerisation. Most of the raw material is acquired and paid for by the customers before production begins.

The company's solicitors are Williams and Co. of Nelson Street, Anytown (D. Williams). The accountants are Drifford and Co. of 20 Print Street, Anytown (M.W.Drifford).

Now the company has found new, larger premises at 34 Thread Street as the enterprise unit had become too small for the expected large turnover. The new building needs some £3,000 spending on it and it will be necessary to spend another £1,200 on more sewing machines.

CASH FLOW

The bank is referred to the company's cash flow for the following year (Figure 21) and should note the following:

(i) Sales are forecast at a realistically achievable level. The company anticipates an average of 33 suits a week, and expectations are that they can get the production up nearly 50 per cent once they are in the new premises.

(ii) The company has found it useful to carry a small stock of finished, unordered suits on sale. A close eye will be kept on the level of stock as the company is anxious not to hold too large a stock.

LOAN REQUIREMENT

The business requires a loan facility of £4,250 to help with the premises and the new machines. From the cash flow projection, it also requires an increased overdraft facility from £3,300 to £5,600, on a short term basis.

Experience has shown that the best plans sometimes take longer than expected, and the business would therefore like to leave open the option of taking the loan of £4,250 over a three-year period. This decision can be made as and when the figures become available. The business will be supplying the bank with monthly results.

It is taking a lease on the new premises, but Fred Lomax has agreed to put up his home as additional security should this be necessary. There is about £16,500 equity in the property after allowing for the outstanding mortgage.

NOTE

This application should be accompanied by Figures 14, 17, 18, 21 and 22 shown on the following pages.

MANUFACTURING INDUSTRY MODEL:
Management Figures

FIGURE 12: PROFIT & LOSS ACCOUNT

	Year 1 £			Year 2 £	%T/over	% G. Profit
Sales	101322	Sales (see Fig 13)		112287	100	
Materials	10000	Opening stock	14000			
	62000	Add Purchases	69000			
	72000	Total	83000			
	14000	Less Closing Stock	17500			
	58000	Cost of Sales		65500		
	43322	Gross Profit		46787	42	100
Wages	16509	Wages		17500		
	4750	Drawings		5000		
	21259	Total		22500		48
Office Expenses	532	Books		564		
	2115	Photocopying		472		
	928	Postages		984		
	1260	Telephone		1336		
	641	Stationery		680		
	1698	Cars		1800		
	450	Typewriters		500		
	7624	Total		6336		14
Building Expenses	2750	Rent		2750		
	583	Rates		688		
	162	Electricity		176		
	120	Gas		130		
	296	Repairs		320		
	3911	Total		4064		9
Finance	266	Bank Interest		350		
	10	Donations		15		
	245	Insurance		275		
	650	Auditors		750		
	1075	Advertising		1150		
	1382	Depreciation		1452		
	3598	Total		3992		7
Misc.	75	Courses		85		
	300	Entertainment		225		
	228	Parking		300		
	500	Staff Adverts		360		
	85	Newspapers		125		
	1637	Other		1965		
	2825	Total		3060		7
	39217	TOTAL EXPENSES		39952		85
	4105	PROFIT BEFORE TAX		6835	7	15

FIGURE 13: ANALYSIS OF TURNOVER

	Product	Amount Invoiced £	Core Total £	%
Core Group 1	A	11085		
	B	15490		
	C	8675		
	D	4761		
	E	4989	45000	40
Core Group 2	F	17517		
	G	7848		
	H	6735		
	I	7200	39300	35
Core Group 3	J	9140		
	K	3559		
	L	1898	14597	13
Core Group 4	M	7901		
	N	2201	10102	9
Misc.	O	3288	3288	3
TOTAL			112287	100

New

	A	B	C	D	E	F	G	H	I	J	K	L	M	N	O	Totals
Department 1	✓✓	✓✓✓✓✓			✓✓✓											0
Department 2	✓	✓✓✓	✓✓✓	✓✓	✓✓											0
Department 3						✓✓	✓	✓✓✓✓	✓✓✓✓							0
Department 4			✓			✓✓✓	✓✓	✓✓✓	✓✓✓✓	✓✓✓✓	✓✓	✓	✓			0
Department 5										✓	✓✓✓	✓	✓		✓✓	0
Totals	0	0	0	0	0	0	0	0	0	0	0	0	0	0	0	0

Invoiced

	A	B	C	D	E	F	G	H	I	J	K	L	M	N	O	Totals
Department 1	2	8			5											15
Department 2	1	5	3	2	2											13
Department 3						2	1	4	7							14
Department 4			1			3	2	3	4	8	2	1	1			25
Department 5										1	3	1	1		4	10
Totals	3	13	4	2	7	5	3	7	11	9	5	2	2	0	4	77

FIGURE 14: FORECAST OF EXPENSES

		Last year £	% Rise	Forecast £	
Income	Sales (see Fig 13)	112287	11	124639	
Materials	Opening Stock	14000		17500	
	Add Purchases	69000	11	76590	
	Total	83000		94090	
	Less Closing Stock	17500		21385	
	Cost of Sales	65500	11	72705	
	GROSS PROFIT	46787		51934	42%
Wages	Wages	17500	9	19075	
	Drawings	5000	9	5450	
	Total	22500	9	24525	
Office	Books	564	5	592	
Expenses	Photocopying	472	5	496	
	Postages	984	5	1033	
	Telephone	1336	5	1403	
	Stationery	680	5	714	
	Cars	1800	5	1890	
	Typewriters	500	5	525	
	Total	6336	5	6653	
Building	Rent	2750	0	2750	
Expenses	Rates	688	5	722	
	Electricity	176	5	185	
	Gas	130	5	137	
	Repairs	320	5	336	
	Total	4064		4130	
Finance	Bank Interest	350	5	368	
	Donations	15	5	16	
	Insurance	275	5	289	
	Auditors	750	5	788	
	Advertising	1150	5	1208	
	Depreciation	1452	–	1525	
	Total	3992	5	4194	
Misc.	Course	85	5	89	
	Entertainment	225	5	236	
	Sundries	2750	5	2888	
	Total	3060	5	3213	
	TOTAL EXPENSES	39952		42715	
	PROFIT BEFORE TAX	6835		9219	

FIGURE 15: FORECAST ANALYSIS OF TURNOVER

	Last Year £	% Rise	Forecast £
Sales Mix			
Core Group 1	45000	10.0	49500
Core Group 2	39300	12.5	44219
Core Group 3	14597	10.0	16057
Core Group 4	10102	11.0	11213
Core Group 5	3288	11.0	3650
Total........................	112287	11.0	124639

FIGURE 16: FIVE-YEAR PLAN

	Year 1 £	%	Year 2 £	%	Year 3 £	%	Year 4 £	%	Year 5 £
SALES									
Core 1	49500	8	53460	7	57202	5	60062	3	61864
Core 2	44219	10	48641	8	52532	12	58836	13	66485
Core 3	16057	8	17342	8	18729	10	20602	11	22868
Core 4	11213	6	11886	6	12599	9	13733	10	15106
Core 5	3650	8	3942	8	4257	8	4598	8	4966
Total..............	124639		135271		145319		157831		171289
MATERIALS									
Opening Stock	17500		21385		22669		24029		25470
Purchases	76590	6	81185	6	86056	6	91219	6	96692
Total	94090		102570		108725		115248		122162
Closing Stock	21385	6	22669	6	24029	6	25470	6	26998
Cost of Sales	72705		79901		84696		89778		95164
Gross Profit	51934		55370		60623		68053		76125
EXPENSES									
Wages	24525	9	26732	9	29138	6	30886	9	33666
Office	6653	10	7318	10	8050	6	8533	6	9045
Building	4130	6	4378	6	4640	6	4919	6	5214
Finance	4194	6	4446	6	4712	6	4995	6	5295
Misc.	3213	6	3406	6	3610	6	3827	6	4056
Total..............	42715		46280		50150		53160		57276
Net Profit	9219		9090		10473		14893		18849
% of Turnover	18		16		17		22		25

FIGURE 17: BUDGET EXPENSES

		Budget	May	Jun	Jul	1/4	Aug	Sep	O
		£	£	£	£	£	£	£	£
Materials	Purchases	76590	4750	5000	4850	14600	5100	5250	57
Wages	Wages	19075	1796	1437	1437	4670	1437	1437	17
	Drawings	5450	524	419	524	1467	419	419	5
	Total	24525	2320	1856	1961	6137	1856	1856	23
Office	Books	592	53	49	49	151	49	49	
	Photocopying	496	41	41	41	123	41	41	
	Postages	1033	86	86	86	258	86	86	
	Telephone	1403	0	0	351	351	0	0	3
	Stationery	714	179	0	0	179	179	0	
	Cars	1890	478	128	128	734	128	128	1
	Typewriters	525	459	0	0	459	0	0	
	Total	6653	1296	304	655	2255	483	304	6
Building	Rent	2750	0	688	0	688	0	687	
	Rates	722	60	60	60	180	60	60	
	Electricity	185	0	0	46	46	0	0	
	Gas	137	0	0	34	34	0	0	
	Repairs	336	0	0	0	0	0	168	
	Total	4130	60	748	140	948	60	915	1
Finance	Bank Interest	368	0	92	0	92	0	92	
	Donations	16	0	0	0	0	0	0	
	Insurance	289	24	24	24	72	24	24	
	Auditors	788	197	0	0	197	197	0	
	Advertising	1208	101	101	101	303	101	101	1
	Depreciation	1525	0	0	0	0	0	0	
	Total	4194	322	217	125	664	322	217	1
Misc.	Courses	89	0	0	45	45	0	0	
	Entertainment	236	118	0	0	118	0	0	
	Sundries	2888	278	222	278	778	222	222	2
	Total	3213	396	222	323	941	222	222	2
TOTAL EXPENSES............... (excluding Purchases)		42715	4394	3347	3204	10945	2943	3514	35

FIGURE 18: BUDGET TURNOVER

	Budget	May	Jun	Jul	1/4	Aug	Sep	
	£	£	£	£	£	£	£	
Core Group 1	49500	2750	3250	3300	9300	3250	3850	3
Core Group 2	44219	2630	3000	3125	8755	3175	3128	3
Core Group 3	16057	975	1325	1250	3550	1150	1250	1
Core Group 4	11213	750	657	950	2357	825	765	
Core Group 5	3650	175	215	210	600	275	235	
Total	124639	7280	8447	8835	24562	8675	9228	

1/2	Nov	Dec	Jan	3/4	Feb	Mar	Apr	TOTAL
£	£	£	£	£	£	£	£	£
30700	6850	6500	7725	51775	8200	8320	8295	76590
9340	1437	2191	1796	14764	1437	1437	1437	19075
2829	419	419	524	4191	419	419	421	5450
12169	1856	2610	2320	18955	1856	1856	1858	24525
298	49	49	49	445	49	49	49	592
246	41	41	41	369	41	41	45	496
516	86	86	86	774	86	87	86	1033
701	0	0	351	1052	0	0	351	1403
358	0	250	0	608	0	0	106	714
1118	128	128	128	1502	128	128	132	1890
459	0	0	66	525	0	0	0	525
3696	304	554	721	5275	304	305	769	6653
1375	0	688	0	2063	0	687	0	2750
360	60	60	60	540	60	60	62	722
92	0	0	46	138	0	0	47	185
68	0	0	35	103	0	0	34	137
168	0	0	0	168	0	168	0	336
2063	60	748	141	3012	60	915	143	4130
184	0	92	0	276	0	92	0	368
0	0	16	0	16	0	0	0	16
144	24	24	24	216	24	24	25	289
394	197	0	0	591	197	0	0	788
606	101	101	101	909	101	97	101	1208
0	0	0	0	0	0	0	1525	1525
1328	322	233	125	2008	322	213	1651	4194
45	0	0	0	45	44	0	0	89
118	0	118	0	236	0	0	0	236
1500	222	222	278	2222	222	222	222	2888
1663	222	340	278	2503	266	222	222	3213
0919	2764	4485	3585	31753	2808	3511	4643	42715

1/2	Nov	Dec	Jan	3/4	Feb	Mar	Apr	TOTAL
£	£	£	£	£	£	£	£	£
350	3950	3750	4250	32300	5250	5750	6200	49500
508	3674	3250	3950	29382	4450	5250	5137	44219
295	1322	1303	1449	11369	1534	1567	1587	16057
861	1021	650	924	7456	1130	1300	1327	11213
400	320	225	335	2280	525	425	420	3650
414	10287	9178	10908	82787	12889	14292	14671	124639

FIGURE 19: ANALYSING PERFORMANCE

	A Annual Budget £	B Actual May £	C Budget June £	D Actual June £	E Variance June (D-C) £	F Year To Date (B+D) £
SALES						
Core Group 1	49500	2750	3250	3450	200	6200
Core Group 2	44219	2630	3000	3200	200	5830
Core Group 3	16057	975	1325	1125	-200	2100
Core Group 4	11213	750	657	875	218	1625
Core Group 5	3650	175	215	127	-88	302
Total Sales......	124639	7280	8447	8777	330	16057
Purchases........	76590	4750	5000	4750	-250	9500
Gross Profit @ 42% of Sales	51934	3057	3547	3686	139	6743
EXPENSES						
Wages	24525	2320	1856	1856	0	4176
Office	6653	1296	304	452	148	1748
Building	4130	60	748	755	7	815
Finance	4194	322	217	196	-21	518
Misc.	3213	396	222	235	13	631
Total.........	42715	4394	3347	3494	147	7888
PROFIT BEFORE TAX	9219	-1337	200	192	-8	-1145

FIGURE 20: QUARTERLY PROFIT & LOSS

		Budget £	Actual £	Variance £
Sales	Core Group 1	9300	9475	175
	Core Group 2	8755	8657	−98
	Core Group 3	3550	3724	174
	Core Group 4	2357	2542	185
	Core Group 5	600	547	−53
	Total Sales...........	24562	24945	383
	Purchases............	14600	15700	1100
Expected Gross Profit @ 42% of Sales...................		10316	10476	160
EXPENSES				
Wages	Wages	4670	4670	0
	Drawings	1467	1467	0
	Total...................	6137	6137	0
Office	Books	151	75	−76
	Photocopying	123	125	2
	Postages	258	275	17
	Telephone	351	345	−6
	Stationery	179	160	−19
	Cars	734	825	91
	Typewriters	459	459	0
	Total...................	2255	2264	9
Building	Rent	688	688	0
	Rates	180	180	0
	Electricity	46	47	1
	Gas	34	38	4
	Repairs	0	15	15
	Total...................	948	968	20
Finance	Bank Interest	92	92	0
	Donations	0	0	0
	Insurance	72	89	17
	Auditors	197	197	0
	Advertising	303	275	−28
	Depreciation	0	0	0
	Total...................	664	653	−11
Misc.	Courses	45	34	−11
	Entertainment	118	165	47
	Sundry	778	756	−22
	Total...................	941	955	14
	TOTAL EXPENSES	10945	10977	32
	PROFIT BEFORE TAX	−629	−501	128

FIGURE 21: CASH FLOW

	May £	June £	Jul £	Aug £	Sep £	Oct £	Nov £	Dec £	Jan £	Feb £	Mar £	Apr £
INCOME												
Debtors/Cash Sale	6115	7095	7421	7287	7752	8357	8641	7709	9163	10827	12005	12324
VAT received	1065	1234	1298	1285	1369	1492	1543	1377	1601	1899	2125	2201
Capital introduced	0	0	0	0	0	0	0	0	0	0	0	500
Other Cash	985	1134	1235	1278	1375	1592	1647	1468	1513	1832	2161	2347
Bank Loan	4250	0	0	0	0	0	0	0	0	0	0	0
Total............(A)	12415	9463	9954	9850	10496	11441	11831	10554	12277	14558	16291	17372
PAYMENTS												
Expenses (Fig 16)	3870	2928	2860	2524	3095	2993	2345	4066	3061	2389	3092	2697
Purchases	4750	5000	4850	5100	5250	5750	6850	6500	7725	8200	8320	8295
Drawings	375	375	375	375	375	375	375	375	375	375	375	375
Loan Repayment	0	120	120	120	120	120	120	120	120	120	120	120
VAT	0	3344	0	0	4011	0	0	4412	0	0	5713	0
Tax	0	0	506	0	0	0	0	0	506	0	0	0
Capital items	4250	0	0	0	0	0	0	0	0	0	0	0
Total............(B)	13245	11767	8711	8119	12851	9238	9690	15473	11787	11084	17620	11487
CASH FLOW (A-B)	−830	−2304	1243	1731	−2355	2203	2141	−4919	490	3474	−1329	5885
BANK BALANCE b/f	−2500	−3330	−5634	−4391	−2660	−5015	−2812	−671	−5590	−5100	−1626	−2955
BANK BALANCE c/f	−3330	−5634	−4391	−2660	−5015	−2812	−671	−5590	−5100	−1626	−2955	2930

FIGURE 22: PROJECTED BALANCE SHEET as at 30 April 19--

	£	£	£
CAPITAL ACCOUNT			
Capital b/f		10416	
Funds introduced		500	
Interest on capital		60	
Profit (as forecast Fig 14)		9159	
Total		20135	
Less -			
Drawings	4500		
Tax	1012	5512	
CAPITAL c/f		———	14623
Fixed Assets			
Lease (at Valuation)	2266		
Less Depreciation	453	1813	
Machinery/Office equipment	3315		
Less Depreciation	663	2652	
Vehicles	2045		
Less Depreciation	409	1636	
TOTAL FIXED ASSETS		———	6101
Current Assets			
Stock		21385	
Debtors		11984	
Cash at Bank		2930	
Total		36299	
Current Liabilities			
Creditors		24341	
Tax		506	
Bank overdraft		0	
Bank loan		2930	
Total		27777	
NET CURRENT ASSETS		———	8522
TOTAL ASSETS			14623

INDEX

Accounts -
  Balance Sheets, 68, 114, 129.
  Profit and Loss Accounts, 17, 23, 25, 30, 52-53, 103, 105, 111, 119, 127.
Advertising, 48, 89-90, 92-98.
Advertising Standards Authority, 93.
Assets, 69-71.

Balance Sheets, 68, 114, 129.
Bank -
  Banking Requirements, 8, 14, 31, 44-45, 72, 99.
  Business Proposition, 7-8.
  Loans, 59-61, 72, 73-76, 78, 100-101, 115-117.
Budgeting -
  Analysis, 46-58.
  Cash Flow, 59-72, 112-113, 128.
  Figures, 105-110, 114, 121-126, 129.
  Forecasting, 32-45.
Businesses (See Also Financing of Business) -
  Name, 93-94.
  Purchase of Existing, 4-6, 11.
  Structure, 9-14.

Cash Flow, 59-72, 112-113, 128.
Clients -
  Debtors, 61-62, 66-67, 71.
  Marketing Information, 84.
  Personal Calling, 90-92.
  Poaching Customers, 4, 5.
  Reliance on Customers, 42-43.
  Target Market, 7, 8.
Companies Act, 13.
Competition, 6, 8, 14, 33, 39, 85.
Computers -
  Spread Sheets, 53-54, 57.
  Use for Stock Control, 24, 44, 50.
Conferences, 84.
Corporation Tax, 64, 78-79.
Creditors, 67, 72.
Customers -
  Debtors, 61-62, 66-67, 71.
  Marketing Information, 84.
  Personal Calling, 90-92.
  Poaching Customers, 4, 5.
  Reliance on Customers, 42-43.
  Target Market, 7, 8.

Debentures, 74-75.
Debtors, 61-62, 66-67, 71.
Depreciation, 22, 48-49, 65.
Distribution, 97-98.
Dividends, 64, 79.

Employees (See Also Wages) -
  Personal Skills in Dealing with, 3.
  Productivity, 40, 43-44, 56-57, 86-87.
Expenses (See Also Wages) -
  Analysis, 16, 18-26, 47-49.

Depreciation, 22, 48-49, 65.
Fixed, 17.
Forecasting, 34-38, 105, 121.
Insurance, 9, 10, 14, 20-22, 37, 48.
Miscellaneous, 22-23, 49.
Office Equipment, 1-2, 19, 35-36, 47, 67.
One Off Costs, 1-2, 17.
Overheads, 13, 17, 56, 88-89.
Pensions, 2, 8, 22, 78, 79.
Premises, 20, 36-37, 47-48.

Financial Times, 6.
Financing of Business -
  Bank Requirements, 8, 14, 31, 44-45, 72, 99.
  Budgeting, 32-45, 46-58, 59-72.
  Cash Flow, 59-72.
  Information, 15-16.
  Liability, 9, 11.
  Loans, 59-61, 72, 73-76, 78, 100-101, 115-117.
  Redundancy Payments, 1-2.
  Sources of Finance, 73-76.
Finished Goods, 24, 68.
Forecasting -
  Analysis, 46-58.
  Budgeting, 32-45.
  Cash Flow, 59-72, 112-113, 128.
  Figures, 105-110, 114, 121-126, 129.
Franchising, 5-6.

Government Assistance, 75.
Grants, 76.
Guarantees -
  Loan Guarantee Scheme, 76.
  Personal, 11-12.

Hobbies -
  As Business Venture, 4.
Holidays, 14.

Income Tax, 10, 11, 64, 72.
Industrial & Provident Societies Acts, 13.
Insolvency Legislation, 12.
Insurance -
  Budgeting, 37, 48.
  Cover, 14, 20-22.
  Credit, 21.
  Health and Life, 21.
  Premises, 21.
  Product or Service Liability, 9, 10, 21.
  Protection of Assets, 20-21.

Letterheads, 93-94.
Liability -
  Financial, 9, 11.
  Insurance, 9, 10, 14, 21.
  Limited Company, 11-12.
  Partnership, 10-11.
  Product or Service, 9, 10, 21.
  Sole Trader, 10.
  Taxation, 77-80.
  Workers' Co-operatives, 12-13.
Limited Companies -
  Insolvency, 12.
  Letterheads, 94.
  Liability, 11-12.
  Personal Guarantees, 11-12.
  Structure, 9, 11-12.
  Taxation, 78-79.
Loans, 59-61, 72, 73-76, 78, 100-101, 115-116.

Machinery -
  Assets, 69-70.
  Depreciation, 22.
Manufacturing Industry (See Also Individual Subjects) -
  Forecasting and Budgeting, 38, 40-41.
  Model, 115-129.
  Pricing, 87-88.

Markets -
   Market Research, 6, 83-84.
   Marketing, 81-99.
   Target Market, 7, 8.

Office Equipment -
   Assets, 69-70.
   Expenses, 1-2, 19, 35-36, 47, 67.
   Leasing, 75.
Overdrafts, 73-74.
Overheads, 13, 17, 56, 88-89.

Partnerships -
   Dissolution, 14.
   Length of Partnership, 13.
   Liability, 10-11.
   Partnership Act 1890, 11.
   Structure, 9, 10-11.
   Taxation, 77-78.
Pastimes -
   As Business Venture, 4.
Pensions, 2, 8, 22, 78, 79.
Periodicals -
   Trade, 6, 33, 84, 95.
Personal Skills, 2-3.
Poaching Customers, 4, 5.
Premises -
   Assets, 69.
   Expenses, 20, 36-37, 47-48.
   Use of Home as Business Premises, 14, 98.
Pricing, 85-89.
Productivity -
   Employees, 40, 43-44, 56-57, 86-87.
Products -
   Attack on Core Business, 39.
   Distribution, 97-98.
   Finished Goods, 24, 68.
   Marketing, 82-99.
   Product Mix Breakdown of Turnover, 26-29, 39, 40-43, 49, 54-55, 56-57.
   Product or Service Liability, 9, 10, 21.
Profits -
   Gross Profits, 50, 52.
   Making a Profit, 15-31, 55-57.
   Minimum Turnover for Viability, 2, 16, 85.
   Profit and Loss Accounts, 17, 23, 25, 30, 52-53, 103, 105, 111, 119, 127.
   Profit Margin, 2, 17-18, 29, 30.
   Sharing between Partners, 14.
Promotion, 89-98.
Publicity, 48, 89-90, 92-98.

Rates, 20, 36, 37, 47.
Raw Materials, 24, 67-68.
Redundancy Payments -
   Investment in Business, 1-2.
Registrar of Companies, 33.
Rent, 20, 36-37, 47.

Salaries -
   Business Owners, 1-2, 8, 14, 63-64.
   Expenses of Business, 17, 18, 35, 38, 43-44, 56.
Sales -
   Closing the Sale, 91-92.
   First Sale, 3, 90.
   Improvement, 66.
   Marketing, 81-99.
   Personal Calling, 90-92.
   Right Kind of Business, 16.
   Sales Mix, 26-29, 39, 40-43, 49, 54-55, 56-57.
Samples, 7, 91.
Service Industry (See Also Individual Subjects) -
   Forecasting and Budgeting, 35-40.
   Model, 100-114.
   Pricing, 85-87.
Shares, 11.

Sole Trader -
  Liability, 10.
  Structure, 9, 10.
  Taxation, 77-78.
Staff -
  Personal Skills in Dealing with, 3.
  Productivity, 40, 43-44, 56-57, 86-87.
Stock -
  Finished Goods, 24, 68.
  Level of Stock, 23-24, 38, 40, 49, 70-71.
  Raw Materials, 24, 67-68.
  Stock Taking and Control, 44, 50, 67-68.
  Stock Turn, 24-25.
Suppliers -
  Creditors, 67.
  Marketing Information, 84.
  Reliance upon Suppliers, 43.

Taxation -
  Corporation Tax, 64, 78-79.
  General, 77-80.
  Income Tax, 10, 11, 64, 72.
  Value Added Tax, 26, 62-63, 64, 89.
Trade Descriptions Act, 93.
Trade Fairs, 84.
Trade Periodicals, 6, 33, 84, 95.
Turnover -
  Analysis, 26-31, 49-50, 104, 106, 120, 122.
  Forecasting, 38-41, 50.
  Minimum for Viability, 2, 16, 85.
  Product Mix Breakdown, 26-29, 39, 40-43, 49, 54-55, 56-57.

Value Added Tax, 26, 62-63, 64, 89.
Vehicles, 19, 38, 70.

Wages -
  Business Owners, 1-2, 8, 14, 63-64.
  Expenses of Business, 17, 18, 35, 38, 43-44, 56.
Workers' Co-operative -
  Liability, 13.
  Structure, 12-13.